Book 2: 61 Days of Barbee's 2018 Index Card Art
With Special Tips and Techniques

But wait, there's more!

Preview the Companion Sketchbook (Book 3) sample at the end of this book with sketches to line and color.

Order your copy today!

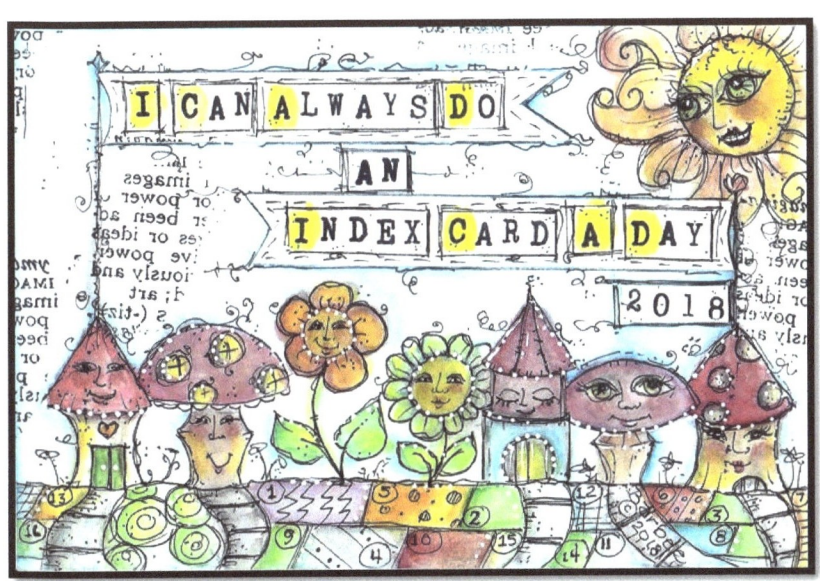

By Barbara Ann Sanders Hauenstein

Copyright 2018© Barbara Ann Sanders Hauenstein.

All rights reserved. No part of this book may be reproduced or sold without permission from the author.

Email the Author: BuzzyBarbee@gmail.com
Subscribe: BuzzyBarbee.blogspot.com

v.20190509

ISBN: 1792882678

Dedication and Acknowledgments

This book is dedicated to those who have inspired me to art every day.

My amazing husband Bruce tops the list. Without his phenomenal planning and publishing skills, I'd still be dreaming about writing a first book. He's my rock!

Our extended family, consisting of four sons, their wives and the children they've been blessed with, are super-positive and uplifting. My talented brother, from whom I learned the magical possibilities of art at a very young age, is also an ongoing inspiration! My wonderful cousins, near and far, have also urged me on and hold a special place in my life, no matter how many miles are between us.

My dear neighbors also encouraged me to continue along my creative path by providing me with role models in the art of living positive, meaningful lives. Even better than this, they've become life-long friends, always there to lend a helping hand and provide good advice.

The driving force behind the Index Card A Day (ICAD) creative challenge, Tammy Garcia (DaisyYellowArt.com), and colorful mixed media trailblazer, Carolyn Dube (AColorfulJourney.com), have provided stepping stones to happy places for many and make this journey fun and easy to enjoy! Each has an awesome, fun website filled with helpful lessons as well as free and paid workshops and a fabulous Facebook Group. These amazing adventurers are "play enablers" and have helped me learn a variety of mixed media techniques that have led me along my creative journey. I hope you'll check them out.

This book is dedicated to the above people as well as my many dear online friends who inspire me to art every day, share what I create and share the processes I use to create. You have all given my art and my life special meaning!

Table of Contents

Reference Chart with Prompt Numbers and Names vii
Summary Collage viii
About the Index Card A Day (ICAD) Creative Challenge ix
Storage and Photos ix
Supply Checklist x
How to Use This Book x
01 for 1 June: ROLLER COASTER 1
02 for 2 June: FIREWORKS 2
03 for 3 June: TILT-A-WHIRL 3
04 for 4 June: FERRIS WHEEL 4
05 for 5 June: QUEUE/LINE 5
06 for 6 June: CAROUSEL 6
07 for 7 June: HAUNTED HOUSE 7
08 for 8 June: ZEBRA 8
09 for 9 June: CHEVRON 9
10 for 10 June: TRAP DOOR 10
11 for 11 June: COFFEE OR TEA 11
12 for 12 June: MAGIC WAND 12
13 for 13 June: COBBLESTONE 13
14 for 14 June: FLAMINGO 14
15 for 15 June: SEA GREEN 15
16 for 16 June: SUPER HERO 16
17 for 17 June: PATH 17
18 for 18 June: SUITCASE 18
19 for 19 June: LEGEND 19
20 for 20 June: GREETINGS FROM 20
21 for 21 June: TREASURE 21
22 for 22 June: SKY 22
23 for 23 June: CASTLE 23
24 for 24 June: THE JETSONS 24
25 for 25 June: TANGERINE 25
26 for 26 June: MEERCAT 26
27 for 27 June: MAGIC CARPET 27
28 for 28 June: GARDEN 28
29 for 29 June: PATISSERIE 29
30 for 30 June: TARO OR PLAYING CARD 30
31 for 1 July: CURTAIN 31
32 for 2 July: COMPASS 32

33 for 3 July: DENIM OR BLUE 33
34 for 4 July: PICNIC 34
35 for 5 July: MOSAIC 35
36 for 6 July: PRETZEL 36
37 for 7 July: POETRY 37
38 for 8 July: PALETTE 38
39 for 9 July: PIXELATED 39
40 for 10 July: PINBALL 40
41 for 11 July: PORTRAIT 41
42 for 12 July: PLATE 42
43 for 13 July: WINDOW 43
44 for 14 July: FRINGE 44
45 for 15 July: CANDYLAND 45
46 for 16 July: TIE DYE 46
47 for 17 July: LOVE 47
48 for 18 July: CAMERA 48
49 for 19 July: LANDSCAPE 49
50 for 20 July: RADIO 50
51 for 21 July: MINT 51
52 for 22 July: POSTAGE 52
53 for 23 July: CASSETTE TAPE 53
54 for 24 July: TIDE POOL 54
55 for 25 July: CIRCUIT OR NETWORK 55
56 for 26 July: TYPEWRITER 56
57 for 27 July: TWISTER 57
58 for 28 July: FAVORITE COLOR 58
59 for 29 July: STAPLE 59
60 for 30 July: WISH 60
61 for 31 July: TELESCOPE 61
PREVIEW OF BOOK 3: COMPANION SKETCHBOOK 62
THANKYOU for Picking Up My Second Book! 63

Reference Chart with Prompt Numbers and Names

Here's a small guide showing mini photos of each Index Card along with the prompt number and name.

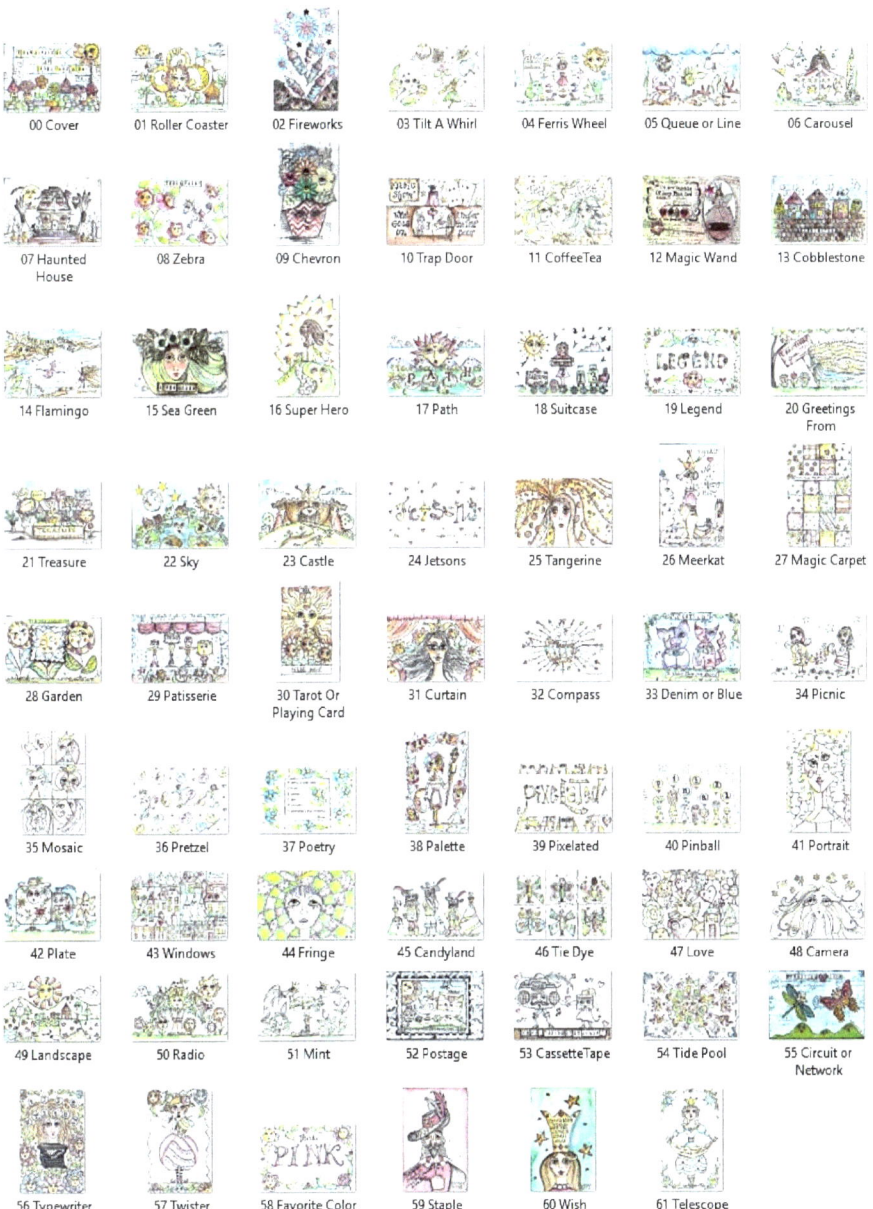

Summary Collage

I used an iPhone (IOS) app to build this collage which has a snippet of each index card. It's another fun way to understand the magnitude of creating a piece of art every day for 61 days!

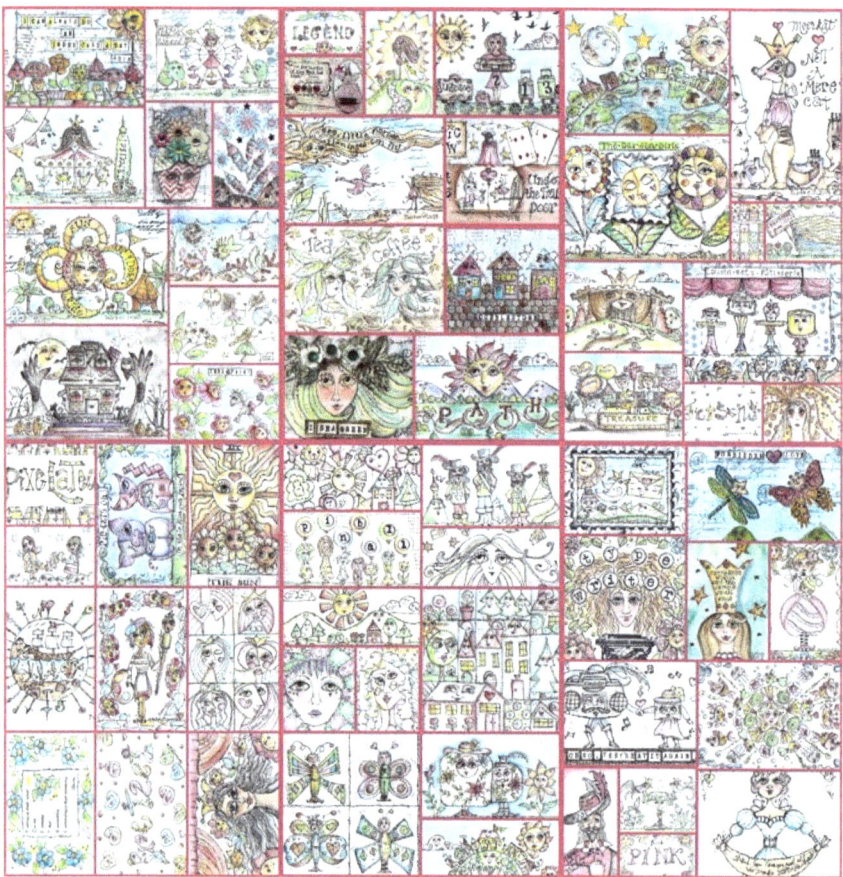

About the Index Card A Day (ICAD) Creative Challenge

I've always enjoyed using index cards to create art, so I was delighted to find Tammy Garcia's "Daisy Yellow Art" website and her creative daily index card challenge online in 2015 where she provides prompts and inspiration.

When I first joined her ICAD Facebook Group, little did I realize I'd be making lasting friendships with other artists from around the world! Many of us keep in touch by creating and posting on Tammy's more general Facebook Group, "Daisy Yellow" throughout the year.

Tammy has other prompt series as well as free and paid workshops on her website that I enjoy. There's a family-friendly atmosphere, and everyone is warm and helpful. There's no pressure to post art, but it's fun to share with others and see what they're doing.

I published my 2017 ICAD collection in "Book 1: 61 Days of Barbee's Index Card Art" earlier this year. This second book provides my 2018 ICAD collection, along with tips and tricks learned along the way. If you enjoy Book 2, please try Book 1 as they have different art, but are both positive and encourage you to try "happy art." There are many styles of index cards created during the challenge. Mine is unique to me but I adore the variety!

Storage and Photos

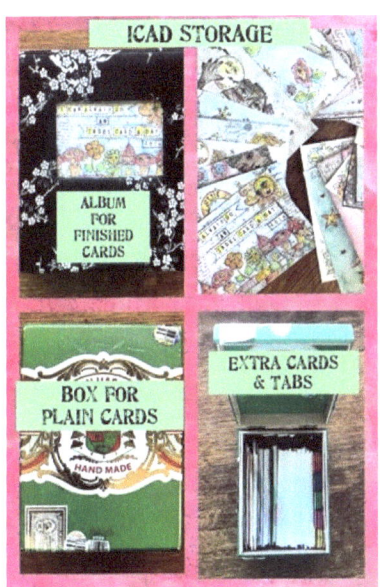

I like to store my index cards in an old wood cigar box rescued from a vintage store in the Midwest.

I divide them with tabbed cards. Once completed, I place them in a photo album from a thrift store that I place on my coffee table for visitors to enjoy.

I use my smart phone to photograph completed cards or scan them into my computer. This collage was created using an iPhone (IOS) app.

Supply Checklist

The supplies you use depend upon the investment you want to make, below are recommendations. You can do a lot with little money by simply gathering items from around your house before visiting a craft store and spending hard earned dollars. By the way, thrift stores are a great place to find supplies and good for the environment!

- ☐ Acrylic and watercolor paint
- ☐ Extra Fine Pens: Gel, Sharpie, Posca paint, Micron 01
- ☐ Gesso
- ☐ Gift or credit cards (old) for spreading media
- ☐ Glitter glue (glitter suspended in glue)
- ☐ Index cards (I used extra thick 4x6 inch)
- ☐ Ink sprays
- ☐ Makeup sponges
- ☐ White glue or glue stick
- ☐ Paintbrushes (Crayola has a good line of them)
- ☐ Paper (junk mail, paper bags, old books, old greeting cards)
- ☐ Pencils
- ☐ Rubber or clear stamps
- ☐ Scissors
- ☐ Stamp pads (permanent and water soluble)
- ☐ Stamps (clear or rubber)
- ☐ Stamps made from household items (bubble wrap, sponges)
- ☐ Stencils
- ☐ Texture paste
- ☐ Regular colored pencils and watercolor pencils

How to Use This Book

Be sure to doodle in the open spaces of these pages and try each of the tips. The more you practice, the more you will learn to be happy with your art. Arting is an action word and a great way to escape life's worries, while still enjoying fun challenges! If you like Book 3 (Companion Sketchbook) sample on page 62, please consider purchasing it. But remember, it's not your mother's coloring book and everyone's result will differ! Instead of plain black and white, it has shades of gray and you can alter and personalize it by adding additional linework. It's an innovative way to practice illustrative sketching and coloring. And don't forget to subscribe to my blog at: BuzzyBarbee.blogspot.com and my "Barbara Hauenstein" YouTube Channel to hear about fun art news and giveaways!

01 for 1 June: ROLLER COASTER

I love adding faces to inanimate objects and enjoyed making one in the center of my roller coaster. I used watercolors, a black permanent fine point pen and a fine point white paint pen.

Tip 1: Add white dots and other white accents with a permanent white paint pen to an almost-finished card to lighten it up and add interest.

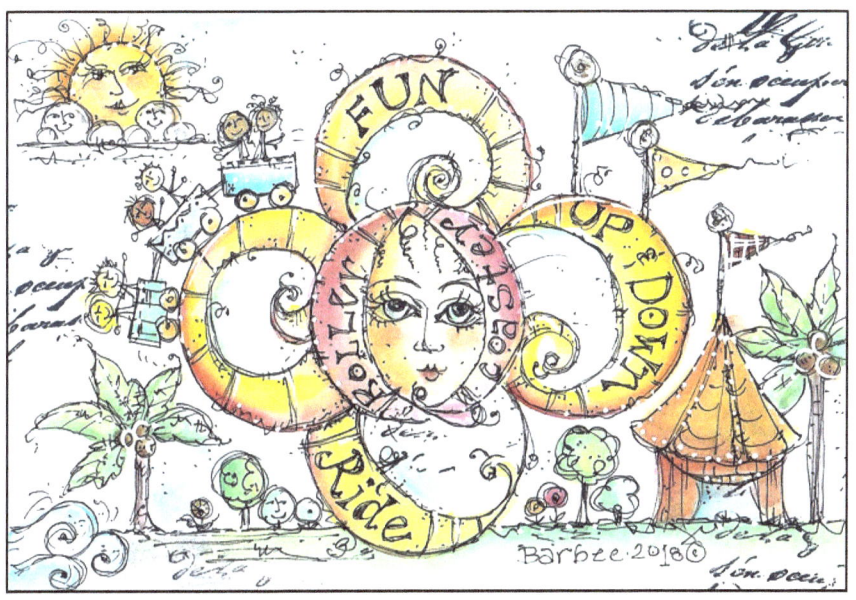

02 for 2 June: FIREWORKS

Lots of fireworks are headed upward and others making beautiful designs in the sky in this piece. All with a sweet, rather mountainous, audience! I began this card by laying out some stencils and slathering texture paste through the stencils to create texture. I then used water color pencils to color the designs. I lined and shaded with a black permanent fine point pen then used a fine point white paint pen to add white highlights.

Tip 2: Use stencils with gesso or texture paste to create 3D designs.

Tip 3: Clip shapes from old book pages and gesso lightly, then adhere to a page to provide interest, texture and layers. Leaving some of the text visible adds interest.

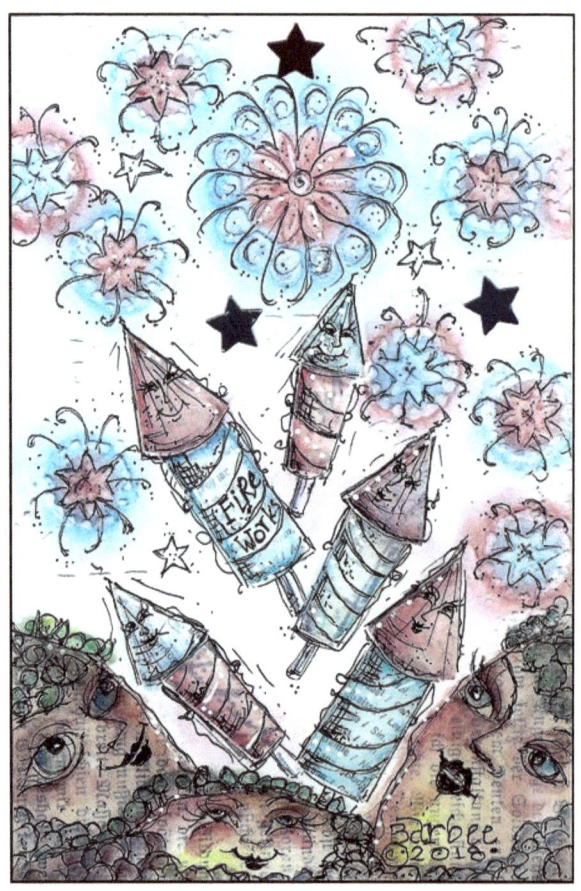

03 for 3 June: TILT-A-WHIRL

My hearing is a bit crazy, did someone say, "Tilt & Whirl?" These little fairies haven't sprouted their wings yet but are joyfully tilting and whirling along with pieces of this dandelion. Notice the sister and brother flowers anxiously but happily waiting their turn to tilt and whirl, too? I hope you like the fairies, do you have a favorite? In researching dandelions, I viewed an amazing short time-lapse video taken over a month showing how the yellow flower sort of implodes, then spits out seeds and opens to a beautiful, full, silver headed dandelion! I used watercolors, a black permanent fine point pen and a fine point white paint pen.

Tip 4: Research prompts to take your mind off daily worries. Add interest to a social media post by using some of the research or adding a sentimental, personalized story to the post.

Tip 5: Use hearts as reference guides to draw whimsical bodies.

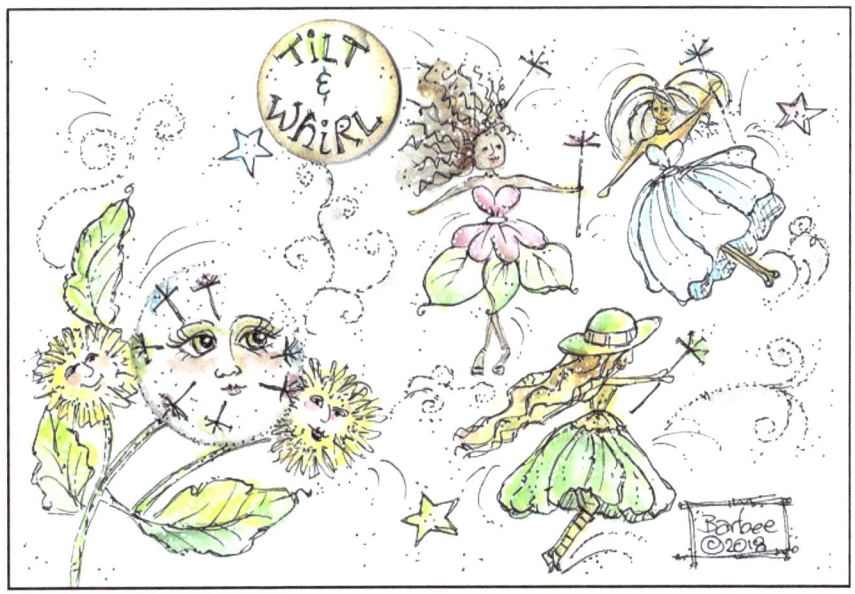

04 for 4 June: FERRIS WHEEL

Several wheels preceded the Ferris Wheel beginning with a 1600s "pleasure wheel" that was turned by several large men. Later, Civil Engineer, George Washington Gale Ferris, Jr. designed a "Ferris" Wheel for the 1893 World's Columbian Exposition in Chicago to meet the challenge to surpass the Eiffel Tower. It had 36 cars with revolving chairs, and was able to accommodate 2,160 passengers at a time, rotating for 20 minutes at a time and carrying 38,000 passengers each day. Ferris claimed that the Exhibition robbed him and his investors of $750,000 and he spent the next two years in litigation. Sadly, bankrupt and suffering from typhoid fever, Ferris died at age 37. The highest Ferris Wheel today is the High Roller in Las Vegas at 550 feet tall which opened in 2014. No need for steel here, my Ferris Wheel on this 4x6 inch index card is held up by an ultra-strong woman! I used watercolors, a black permanent fine point pen and a fine point white paint pen. I added some texture using script stamp, bubble wrap and a stamp pad.

Tip 6: Lightly stamp text and bubble wrap or other household objects on a card to add interest and create a mixed media project.

Tip 7: Use different colored ink stamp pads to match themes or create moods on cards. Use permanent ink, if you don't want the stamped image to run if you'll be using other media that's wet.

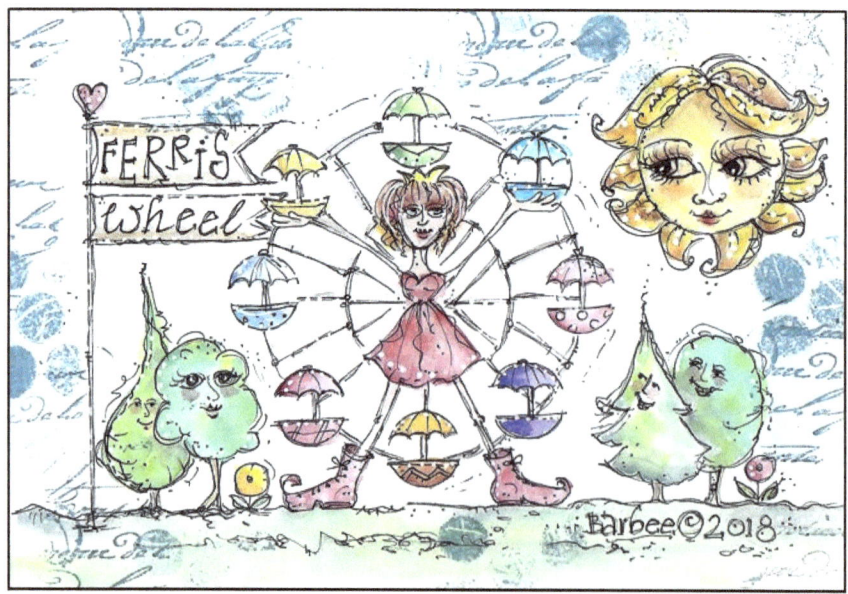

05 for 5 June: QUEUE/LINE

I love to think about unique ways to creatively meet the challenge posed by these fun prompts and I wanted to do a painting of the ocean food chain for this one depicting the queue that sealife must form to survive. My grandiose plans showing a long queue of characters queue'd up in this important food chain quickly dwindled down to these 3 when faced with the reality of size restrictions of my 4x6 inch index card. I used watercolors, a black permanent fine point pen and a fine point white paint pen. I added some texture using a compass stencil and a background stencil with a blue stamp pad, accented with a bit of dark brown and black which was in the foam ink applicator - don't you love those little surprises!

Tip 8: Use removable 3-dimensional tape to add titles or text you want to be able to remove in order to use your card for something else later. I punched a circle and hand wrote: "IN THE QUEUE" then attached it using 3-D sticky tape. Later, I can remove the circle and use the index card to create birthday and anniversary cards!

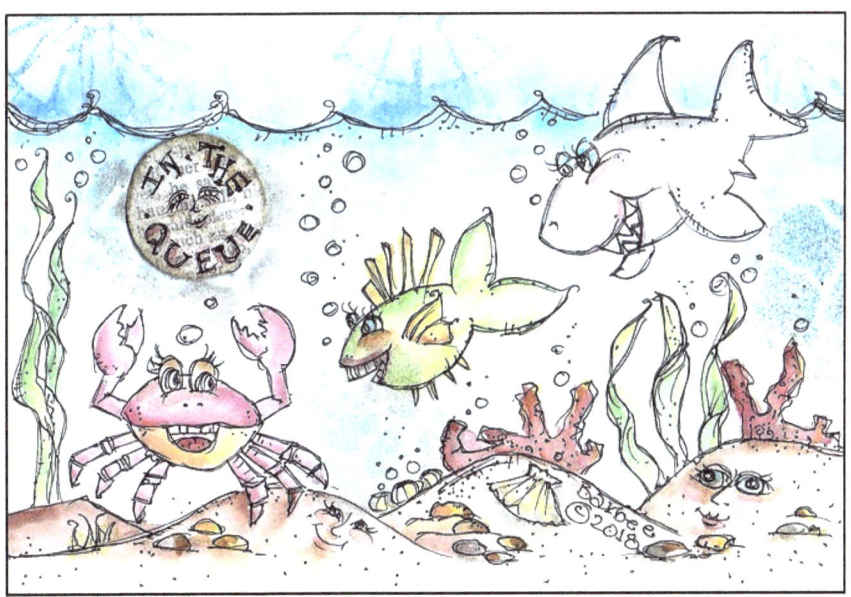

06 for 6 June: CAROUSEL

I love horses soooo much but struggle to draw ones I am happy with so decided to create a horse-free carousel to get this piece done and move on to the next prompt. I had to do this because I found myself stopping on this card too long, worried that my horse would be awful. I felt I could draw a simple song bird, mouse and chicken, so stuck with them. Have no doubt horse-lovers, I am continuing to practice horses and will post a wonky horse one day that I'm happy with! I used watercolors, a permanent fine point black pen and a fine point white paint pen.

Tip 9: Add hand-written words to cards to label things, add interest and practice lettering techniques.

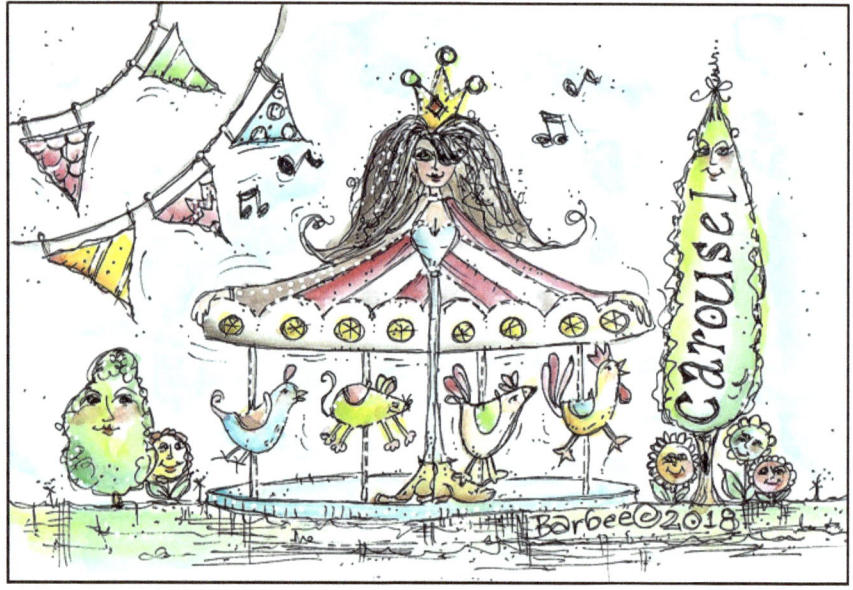

07 for 7 June: HAUNTED HOUSE

I enjoyed adding lots of faces and two cats to this haunted house. The scary arm-trees were a must, along with that full moon. The owl is enjoying the show and the pumpkins add the final touch. I used watercolors, a fine point black permanent pen and fine point white paint pen.

Tip 10: Use a brush to apply water to a background then add watered-down watercolor for a unique watercolor technique that yields a lovely, soft background.

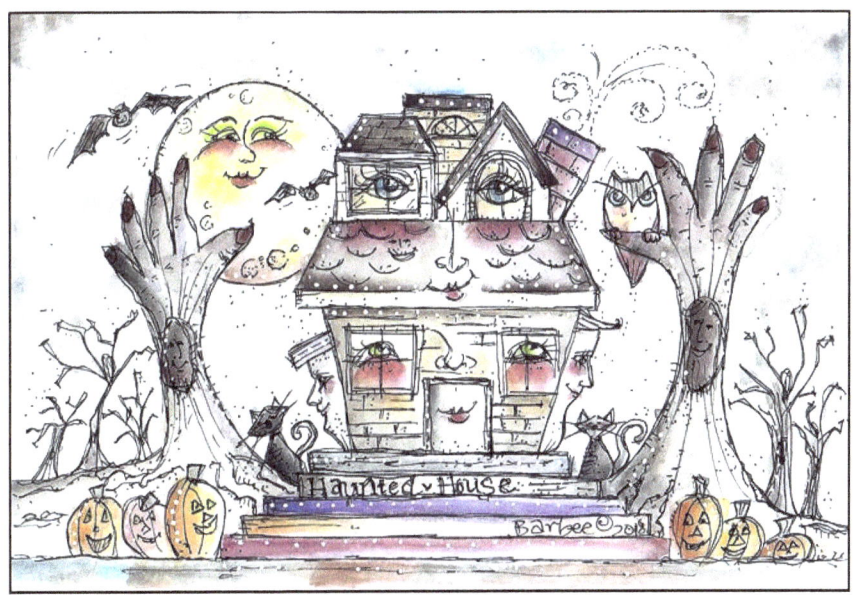

08 for 8 June: ZEBRA

I wasn't excited about doing a zebra, however, another fairy seemed fun, so I created a zebra fairy with lots of pink flowers. One of the flowers became the perfect tutu, however, just like the tutu-d zebra I did a while back, this zebra fairy asks: "does it make my butt look big?!?" (haha!) I used watercolors, a fine point black permanent pen and fine point white paint pen.

Tip 11: If not sure what to do, add wings to a subject (like this zebra) to spruce up the card. Adding fun clothing like a tutu is always a good idea, too, and will keep you giggling as you create!

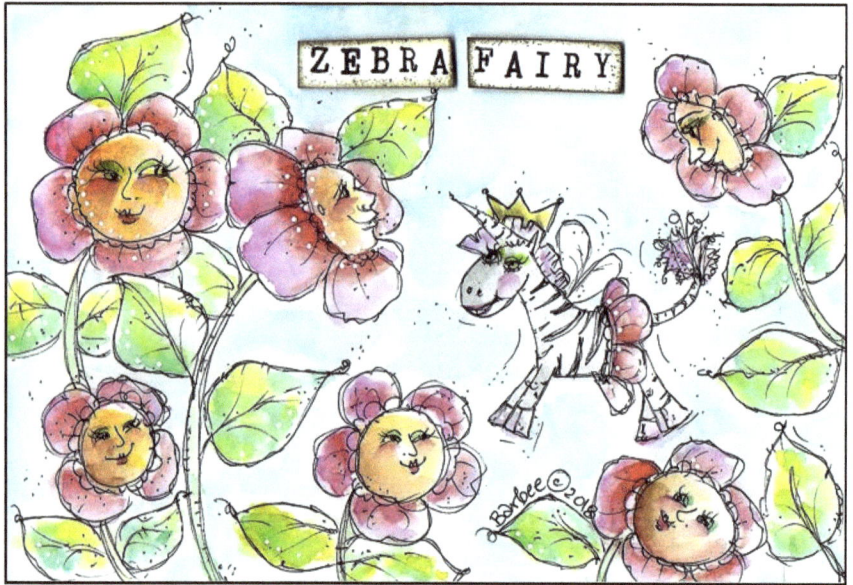

09 for 9 June: CHEVRON

This vase with flowers is a collage of gesso'd, then stenciled (with stamp pads) book pages plus some metal flowers and gems. I also added some linework with a fine point pen. Lastly, I added accent dots all around with a fine white paint pen.

Tip 12: Add embellishments like paper, silk or metal flowers and gems to a card to add an unexpected dimension.

Tip 13: If you're at a loss for things to do, draw a simple vase and / or flowers and / or a face. These are my "go to" subjects when I can't think of anything to draw.

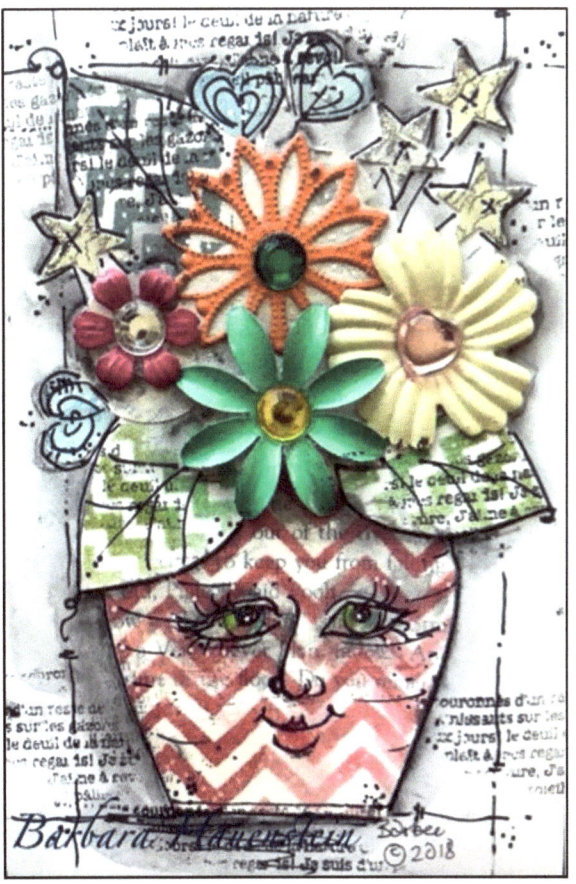

10 for 10 June: TRAP DOOR

Do you ever wonder what's going on at the magician's table? And UNDERNEATH that magicians table? Well here's my take on it. I think the magic bunny and magic bird are having martinis, margaritas and FUN down there. They've fallen in love and so are looking into each other's eyes. I know it's not quite to scale but I'm finding it's hard to fit everything into my 4x6 inch index cards so sometimes fudge the scale on purpose to emphasize specific details The little miniature cards were glued on and came from a dear friend who I swapped artist trading cards with (I love ephemera - thank you Susan!). I used watercolors, a fine point black permanent pen and fine point white paint pen. I also added a couple accents with regular colored pencils.

Tip 14: Think of humorous, unexpected situations to portray in a card.

Tip 15: Use small bits of ephemera to add dimension and interest to a card.

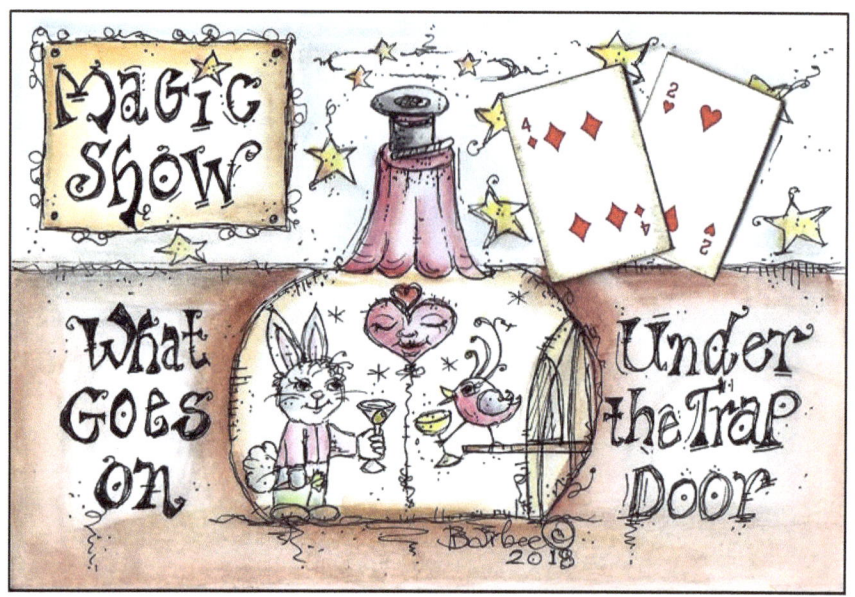

11 for 11 June: COFFEE OR TEA

I've never understood how people could like EITHER coffee, tea, coke OR something else similar as I like them all! They make tea from all different things - regular "tea" leaves or licorice or chrysanthemum or better yet, a synergistic blend for every purpose. I love the relaxing effects of chamomile and just found some tea called tension tamer! I also love soft drinks AND foo-foo coffee. That is coffee adorned with different syrups, cream and spices, like caramel macchiato syrup, half and half and nutmeg or cinnamon spice. I added leaves to these sweet, wide-eyed-fairy-heads to indicate tea and coffee but had a hard time seeing the difference in the plants in reference photos on the internet and didn't want to take more time since I needed to catch up doing more daily prompts, so please join me in doing some make believe that one wide-eyed-fairy-head has tea-leaf hair while her bestie has coffee-leaf hair! There's lots of energy surrounding these two because they drank a lot of these fabulous drinks! I used watercolors, a fine point black permanent pen and fine point white paint pen.

Tip 16: Add leaves, stars, and /or flowers as well as hand-written text when you're having a hard time figuring out what to draw or collage on a card.

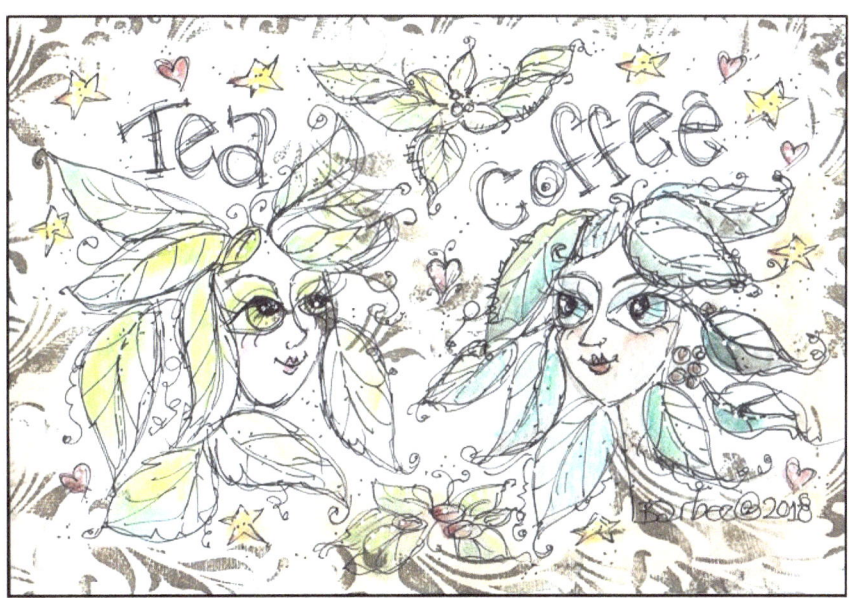

12 for 12 June: MAGIC WAND

I still love to watch the old Wizard of Oz movie around the holidays, so I knew I wanted to portray the magic wand of Glinda, the good witch from that movie for this prompt. I glued a gem flower with pearl on top of that extra-large star-tipped wand to add more glitz and extra fab dimension. I used a fine point black permanent pen to add some doodles. I used a wonderful flourish background stamp to add texture around the outside part of the card and added gems and little pearls from a local store. I added a metal piece that says "Believe" as well. During my research, I found several quotes by Glinda so added one to this card. I was surprised by the encouraging, wise things she said!

Tip 17: Use photos from junk mail, old books or magazines on cards.

Tip 18: Create poems or add quotes to cards. This is especially helpful if you're not able to think of an idea for the prompt.

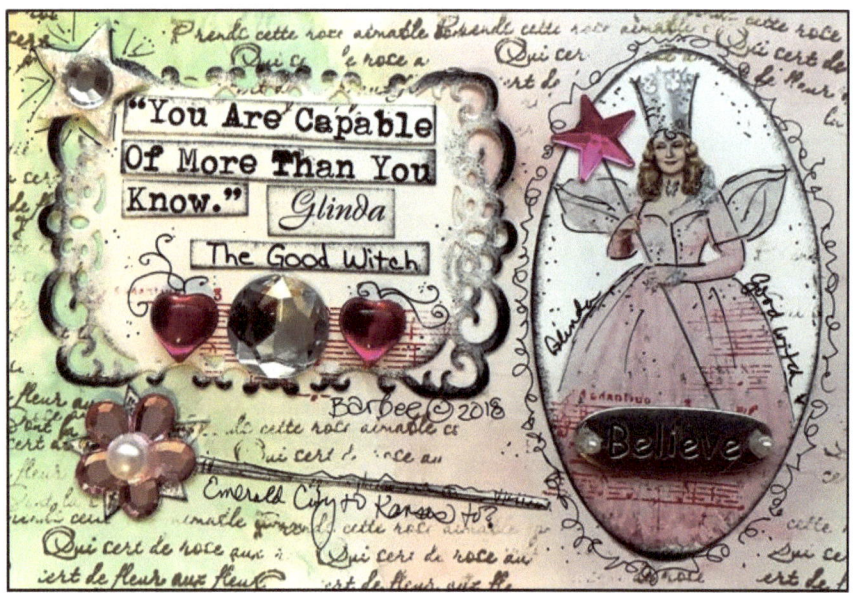

13 for 13 June: COBBLESTONE

I wanted to draw cobblestones and houses but decided to use stencils and texture paste from my friend, Martina's, online store, My Rusty Crown (excellent items and prices!), for cobblestones and stars. I used some text, ledger and music paper to make the houses, but the designs got overcome by gesso and watercolor, so you can't see them! After adding details with a fine point black pen, I added some white accents with a fine point white paint pen. I colored the cobblestones with different colors of watercolor and painted a few stars with white acrylic paint. I also added some text with a stamp here and there. I made the word "cobblestone" with an old rotary alphabet stamp and used removable tape to adhere it to the card. After taking this picture, I replaced it with words that will enable me to print photos of the card to use for greeting cards. So, it now says "home sweet home." I like to be able to re-use my index card art for other things.

Tip 19: Use texture paste through a stencil to get a 3D look. Use watercolors, watercolor pencils or acrylic paint to color it. Use pen to outline some of the patterns, if desired.

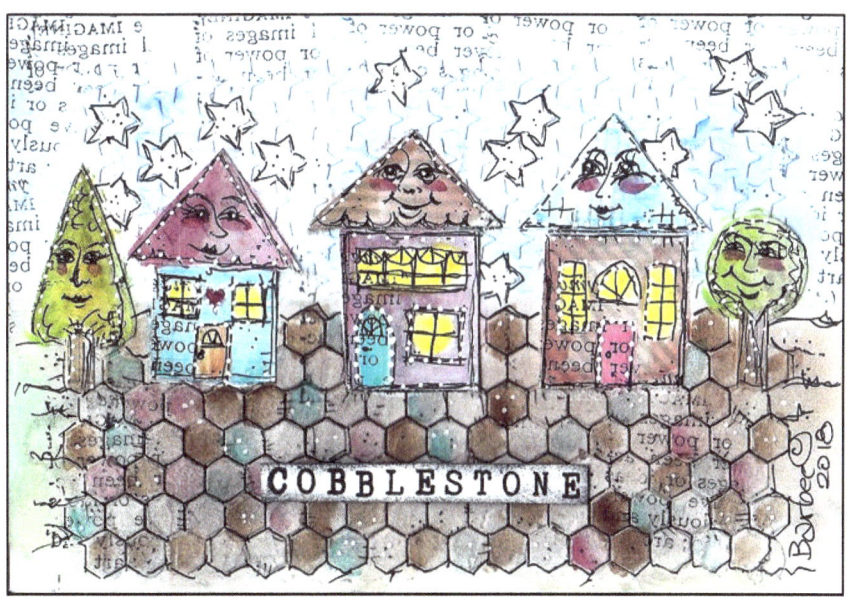

14 for 14 June: FLAMINGO

I wanted to do a detailed vintage girl for this but was behind with my daily cards so drew this scene instead since I felt like it was quicker. I posted the little statement to my alter-ego, Little Barbee, because I used to wonder if flamingos really could fly since we typically don't see them flying. I love flamingos so much, probably cuz they're pink, haha! I used a liner pen to draw the design then painted it with watercolors. I added a little colored pencil here and there to intensify the colors with a variety of colored pencils. I added white accents with a fine point white paint pen and stamped a script stamp on the background.

Tip 20: Don't attempt perfection when drawing. Simple, sketched figures give the idea of anatomy, without necessarily being anatomically correct.

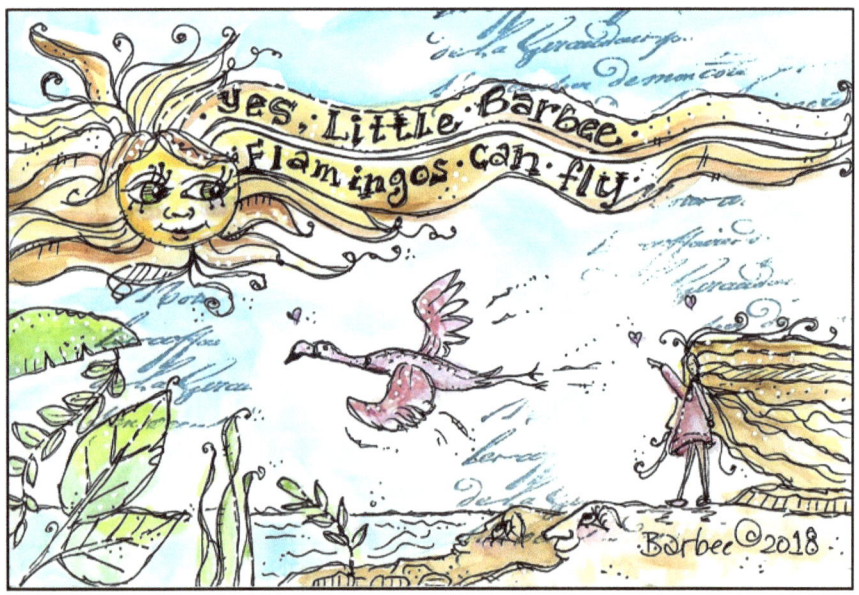

#15 for 15 June: SEA GREEN

After coloring so much green on this card, I felt that the words, "I SEA GREEN" were quite appropriate. This lady looked a little bare after I drew her with a fine point pen and colored her with watercolor pencils, so I glued on leaves – some cut from a sheet of music, others from an old book. I added shading with a black watercolor pencil around the leaves to make them stand out from her hair. I glued three silk flowers to the leaves and added green gems to the middle of each flower. I also added little bubbles around the outer, bluish sea as well as some random text stamp with a green stamp pad.

Tip 21: Use a play on words and add it as a feature on the card to make the prompt (and card) more interesting.

Tip 22: Use die-cuts from music paper and / or text. Books, magazines and newspaper all provide excellent sources. Paper can be gesso'd or painted to add a vintage look to a card.

Tip 23: Use different colors of stamp pads that match other colors on the card to stamp designs. This adds cohesiveness.

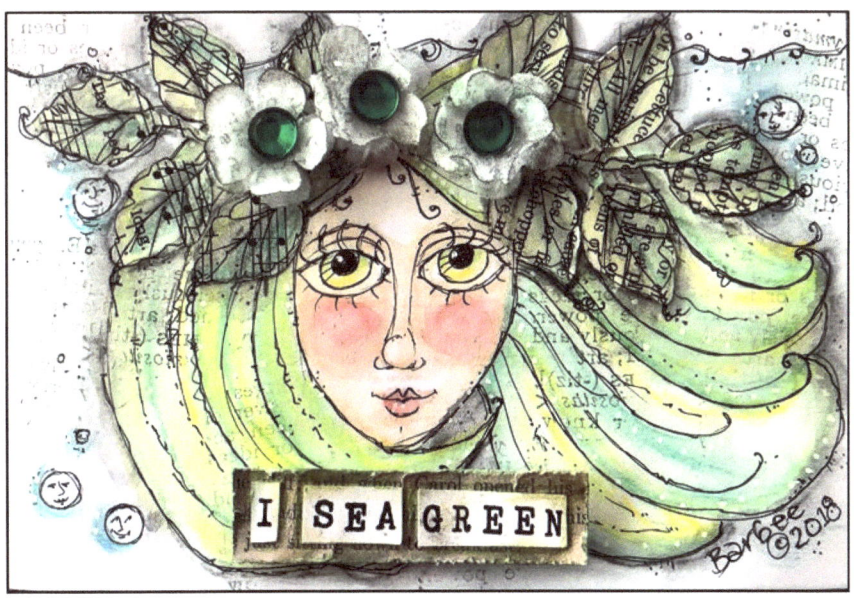

16 for 16 June: SUPER HERO

Mothers get my vote for being real-life superheroes! I enjoyed making this little mom with big hair and a long flowing Super-Mom Cape! I used a black fine point permanent liner pen, watercolor pencils and a fine point white paint pen.

Tip 24: Use an old make-up sponge to apply ink from a stamp pad around the edges of a card or cutout to create definition and make cuttings stand out from back ground.

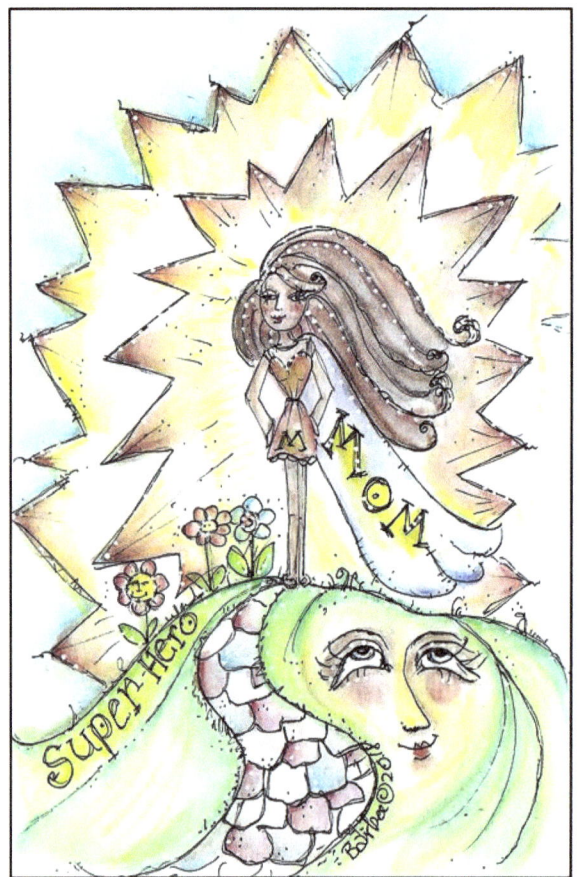

17 for 17 June: PATH

Here's my little path. And what I've discovered about my path is that it's better than a walk in the park. Guess that's why they call it a path and not a walk in the park. But I sure enjoy everything in my life because I love it all so much! That's why sometimes my path goes in circles - because I want to enjoy special moments for longer than a moment. I used a permanent black fine point pen, watercolor pencils and a fine point white paint pen. I finished by stamping a numerical stamp onto the background because I felt it needed something else.

Tip 25: Pay attention to little times of great joy in your life and enjoy them for longer than a moment!

Tip 26: Be positive in writing a post about your art. Foster a positive attitude in yourself (and others) by posting happy thoughts and leaving the negative ones behind. You and the reader will enjoy the post, and your day, far more.

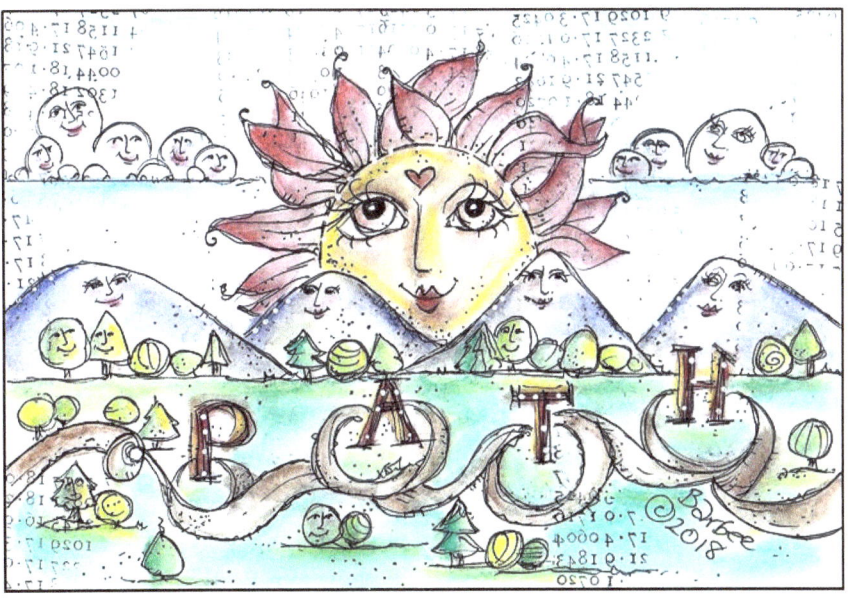

18 for 18 June: SUITCASE

Suitcases, just like us, come in all shapes and sizes. My oldest memory of suitcases was the brown grainy leather ones my mom and dad bought when they married in post-World War II Europe as they prepared to travel back to the U.S. A dark-haired handsome air force sergeant bringing his beautiful young immigrant bride back home to live in the country he cherished so much. Many suitcases have come and gone since then, but I'll always cherish those original brown leather ones with decals from many places that served us so well for so long. I used a black fine point permanent pen for this creation on a 4x6 index card, watercolor pencils and a fine white paint pen. I finished by stamping some images of birds in the sky, because I felt it was too bare.

Tip 27: Incorporate personal stories that touch the heart in a positive way. Writing about fond memories makes the artist and the reader happier.

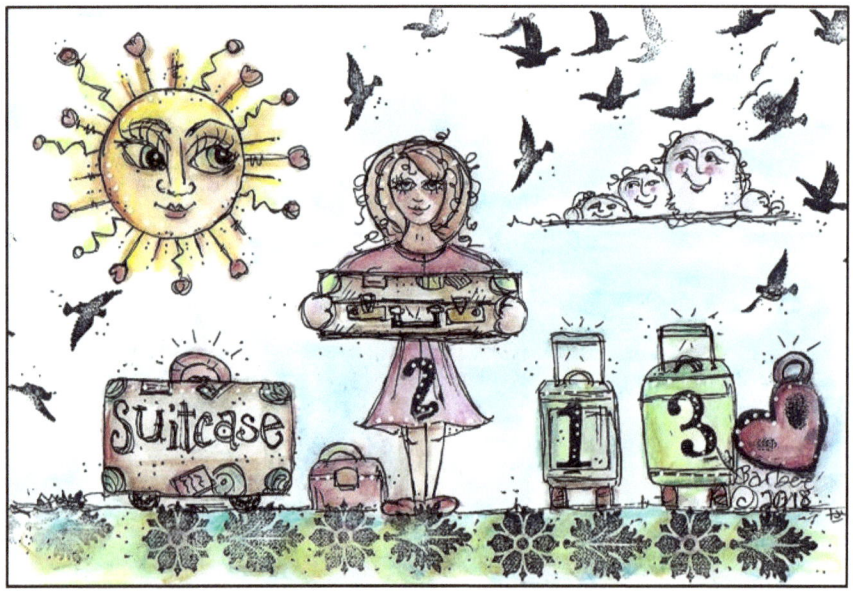

19 for 19 June: LEGEND

I kept thinking up complex plans for this prompt, but since I was in my usual rush to get a card done decided to create some fun lettering to spell out the prompt instead. I enjoyed giving some personality to the little characters. Adding the bunny details on the "E" was a last thought that caused me to chuckle! Which is your favorite character? I used a black permanent fine point pen and watercolor pencils then finished it off with a few dotty marks using a fine point paint pen.

Tip 28: Keep things simple. Creating a work of art every day doesn't allow much time to plot and execute complex plans. So, it's best to reign in your ideas by simplifying if you feel stressed that you're getting behind.

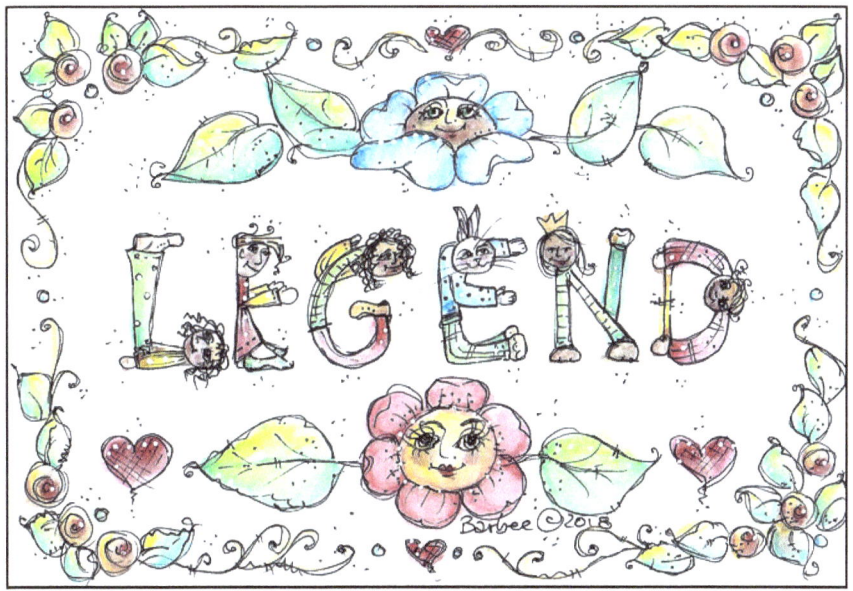

20 for 20 June: GREETINGS FROM

I listed places from which artists post to FaceBook art groups that I frequent on this 4x6 index card for the prompt "Greetings from." I enjoyed writing the places in this girl's flowing hair and made her multi-color dress flow with the same ripple effect as her hair. I used a permanent fine point black pen, watercolor pencils and a white fine point paint pen.

Tip 29: Use ICAD to practice processes. I practiced with watercolors and watercolor pencils on this girl's dress. It was fun using blue and green there and watching them intermingle!

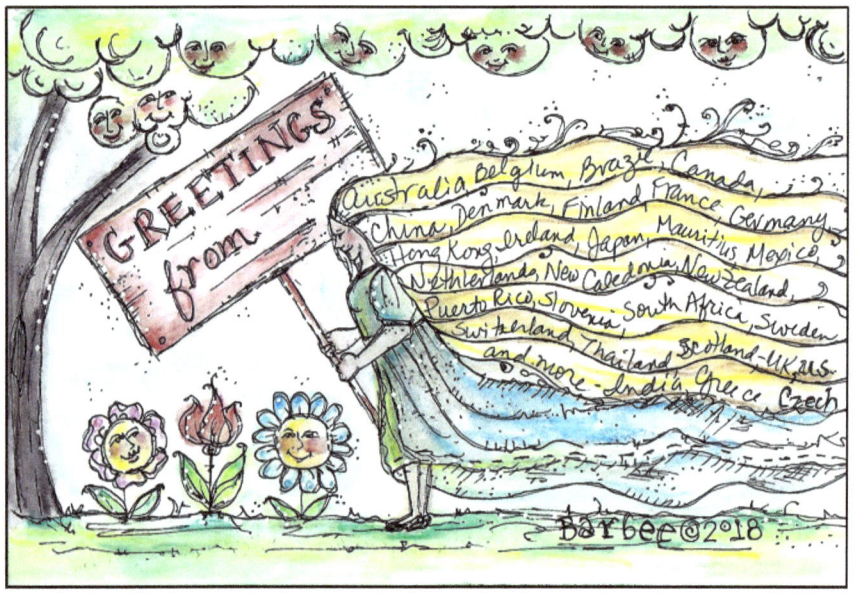

21 for 21 June: TREASURE

This topless treasure box is overflowing with some of the treasures that are important to me: faith, family, friends, food, technology (my beloved devices), health, nature, science, income, animals, home, travel, and art. I used a permanent fine point black pen, watercolor pencils and a fine point white paint pen. After posting this, I received a sweet message from a fellow ICADian showing me ("Barbee") in a treasure box too! Wow, such nice people in the group.

Tip 30: Leave a margin around the card to allow for all of it to be placed in a photograph. I cut it a bit too close when I added the palm tree at the left!

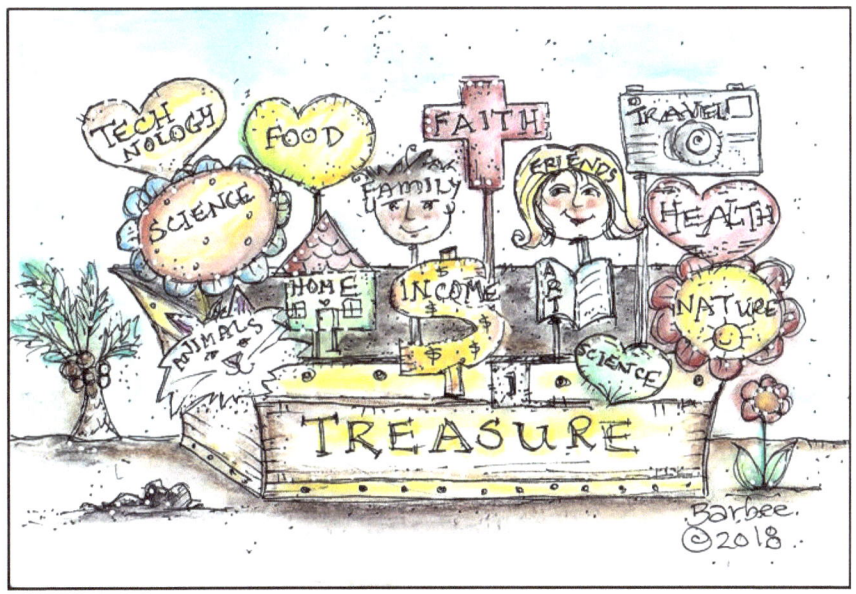

22 for 22 June: SKY

This sky has both a sun, moon and Mother Earth cut from book paper, lightly gesso'd, then glued on with white glue. It also has stars cut from yellow paint chips. I love drawing houses and animated trees as well as happy suns and moons! I used a permanent fine point black pen, watercolors and a fine point white paint pen.

Tip 31: Use shapes cut out from paint chips in your art.

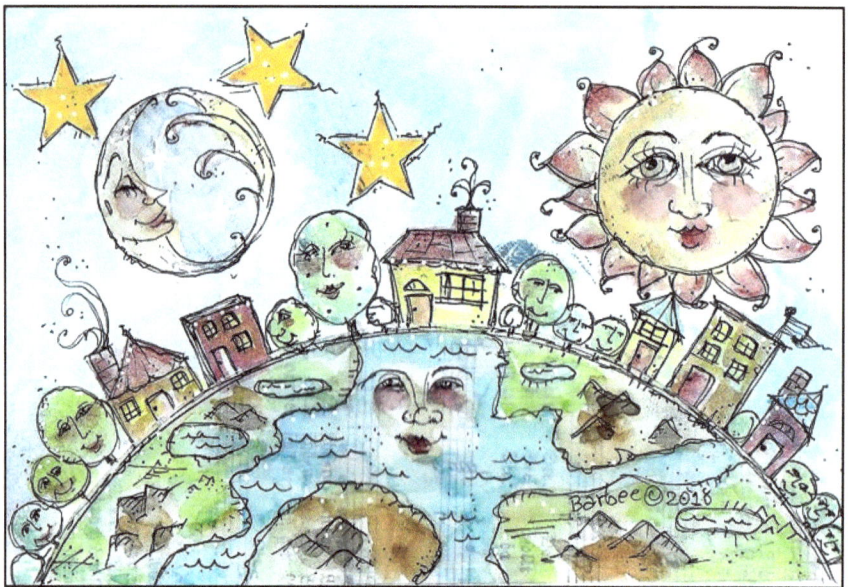

23 for 23 June: CASTLE

I love castles and wanted to draw one so was excited that Tammy had included this as a prompt! My castle is in a great mood, as are the clouds and trees. I've been playing with watercolors lately and, although index cards don't provide the best substrate for them, I've been learning to blend and control them. It's fun to continue my journey with this fabulous media. I'm surprised that different brands of watercolor layout different looking effects, but I'm enjoying the challenge of finding the best ways to use them as well as how to use my fine-line black permanent markers and white paint pen to accentuate them.

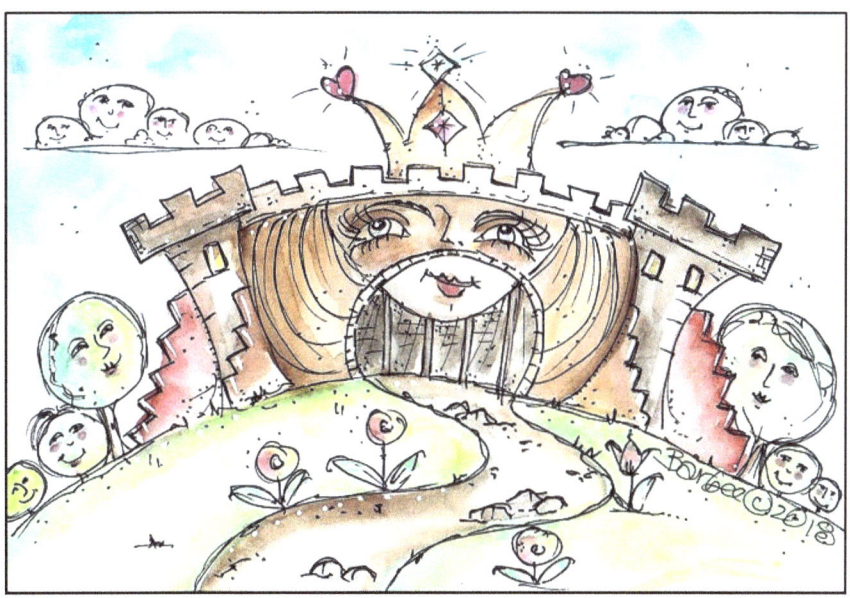

24 for 24 June: THE JETSONS

My formula for catching up during ICAD, so that I made 61 cards in 61 days, is to simplify some cards till I catch up. I also like to write the prompt and make interesting letters as it presents a challenge but is quicker than some of my other ideas. I enjoyed watching the Jetsons but thought it would take too long to draw something that resembled the entire cartoon characters so instead decided to portray objects in their lives. I used a permanent fine point black pen and watercolor pencils.

Tip 32: Play with the letters of words by embellishing them to give them a unique flair. When strapped for time, use the prompt or other word for a quick card.

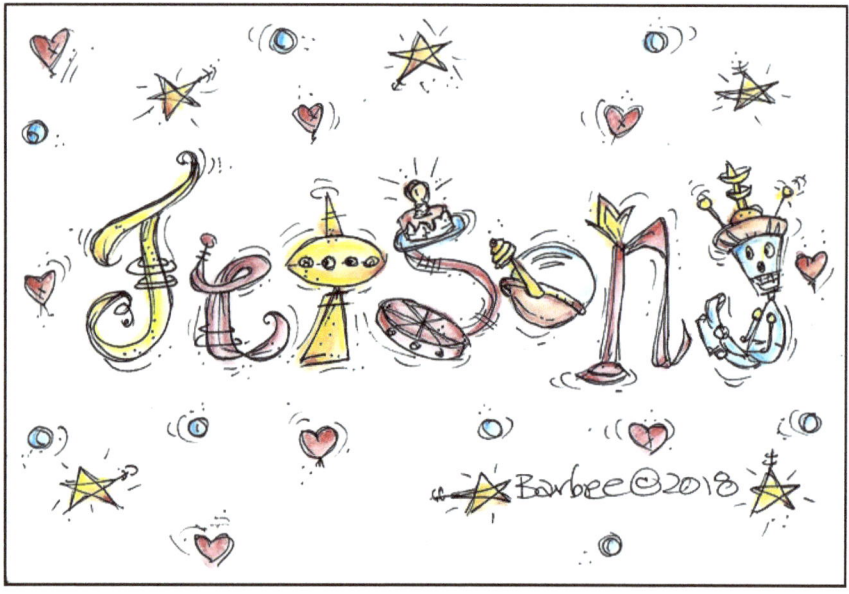

25 for 25 June: TANGERINE

I got stuck on this prompt so initially passed it by and went on to the next prompt. Freezing because no creative ideas come can stop me dead in my tracks, so I move past them initially. I keep thinking about them anyway and let them grow like a seed in my mind till I come up with something. As we neared the end of this wonderful daily challenge (about day 54 on 24 July – only 7 days to go), I went back to my old standby – a face with doodles, of course! I used a permanent fine point black pen, watercolor pencils and a fine point white paint pen.

Tip 33: Add random patterns to large white areas to fill them with delight.

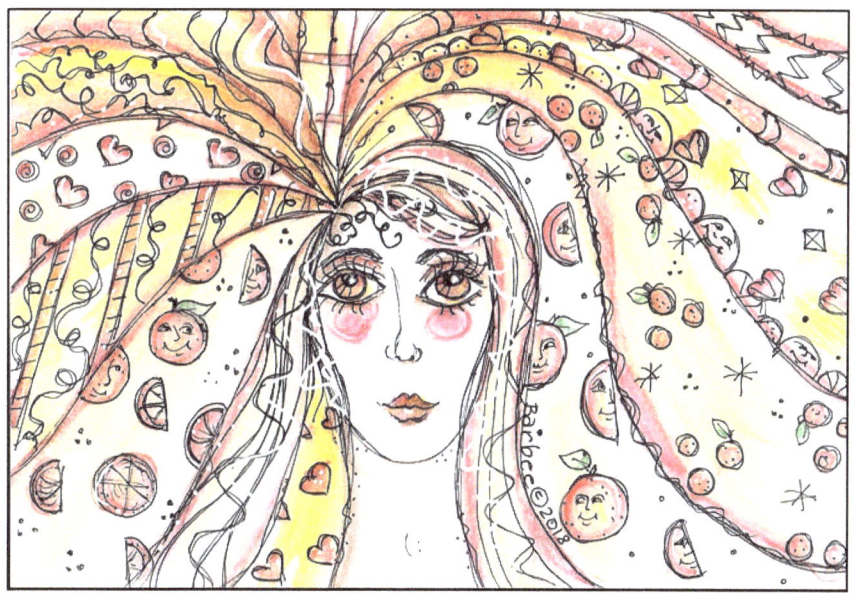

26 for 26 June: MEERCAT

This little Queen Fairy Meerkat is definitely NOT a MERE cat, haha! The prompt was for 26 June, but I did it about day 55 on 25 July with only 6 days to go until ICAD ended. I initially procrastinated because I felt intimidated by the thought of drawing a meerkat since it's outside the realm of my usual art, but eventually I took the chance and it wasn't as difficult as I thought it would be. Do you see the myriads of other meerkats paying homage in the distance? You can't see one without many far behind. Doing this challenge bolstered my confidence and I now try to draw everything! That doesn't mean I think I can draw everything perfectly, but I believe I'll be able to sketch things whimsically and be happy with my art. The key is being able to identify what we don't like so we can change it, even though that sometimes takes a long time.

Tip 34: View subjects in terms of shapes. Use words if nothing else comes to you, and you'll be able to do something every day.

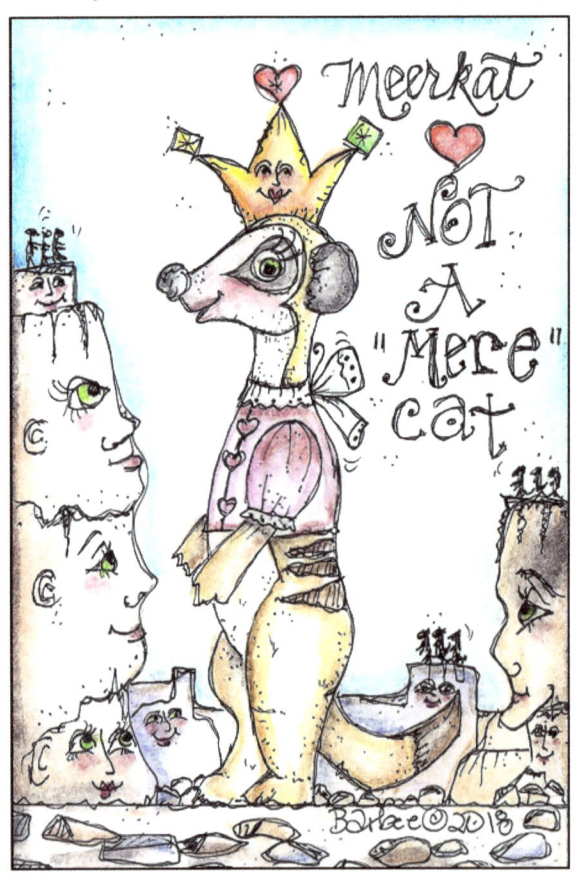

27 for 27 June: MAGIC CARPET

I wanted to do a patriotic red, white and blue quilt in celebration of the 4th of July as well as my friend, Phyllis', birthday in June and this prompt seemed perfect for my "Americana Magic Carpet Quilt." Think of how many quilts have been made from remnants of ancestors' lives and accompanied dear ones from birth or wedding all their lives and then probably passed along to another. Quilts certainly are Magic! This one is dedicated to Phyllis, whom I've known and been friends with, most of my life. She's an amazing quilt-artist! Thank you, Phyllis, for enriching our lives with your gorgeous quilts and wonderful conversation every Friday afternoon. And Happy Birthday! I used watercolor pencils, black permanent fine point pen, white paint pen.

Tip 35: Think about using your art for a card for a friend. This will give you more ideas and encourage you to complete the daily art.

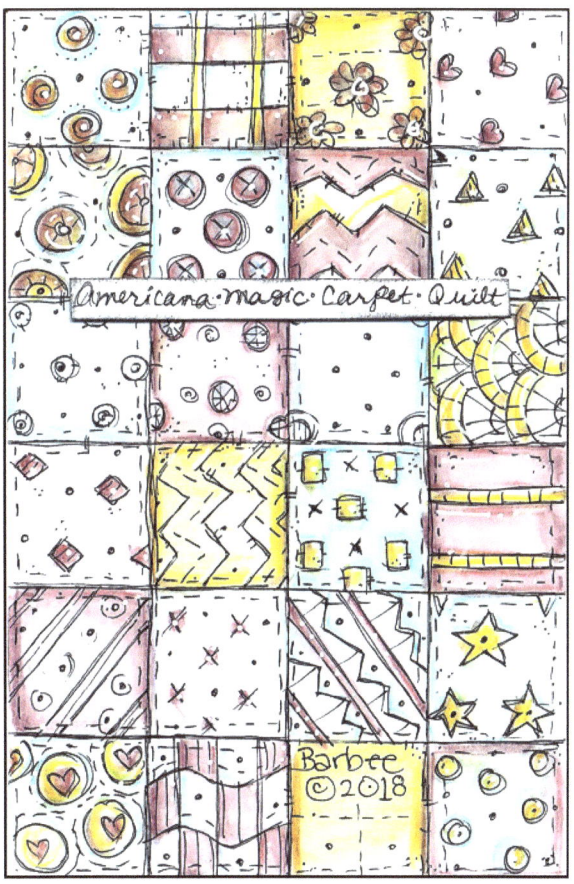

28 for 28 June: GARDEN

I call this one, "The Garden Sisters!"

I started this card by adhering old book pages and music sheets that I'd clipped into flowers and the bottom grass shapes. The original faces ended up becoming too dark and it was difficult to see the ink details on them because the text on the book page was too dark and interfered with the face. So, I pulled those faces off and re-did them by adhering and coloring lighter ones. When doing these cards, I am reminded that all brands of permanent pens must be checked on different media to make sure they don't smear. For instance, the micron fine tip black pen is labeled as permanent but when used on a book page that's been covered with white acrylic paint, it smeared. Because of this, I used plain cardstock circles for the faces, which worked much better. The paint and gesso you use can yield different results, so it's best to try different brand pens with different brand paints and gessos. I used watercolors and watercolor pencils along with that black micron pen.

Tip 36: Try out pens with different brands of paint, gesso's and backgrounds to make sure they don't smear before using on your card.

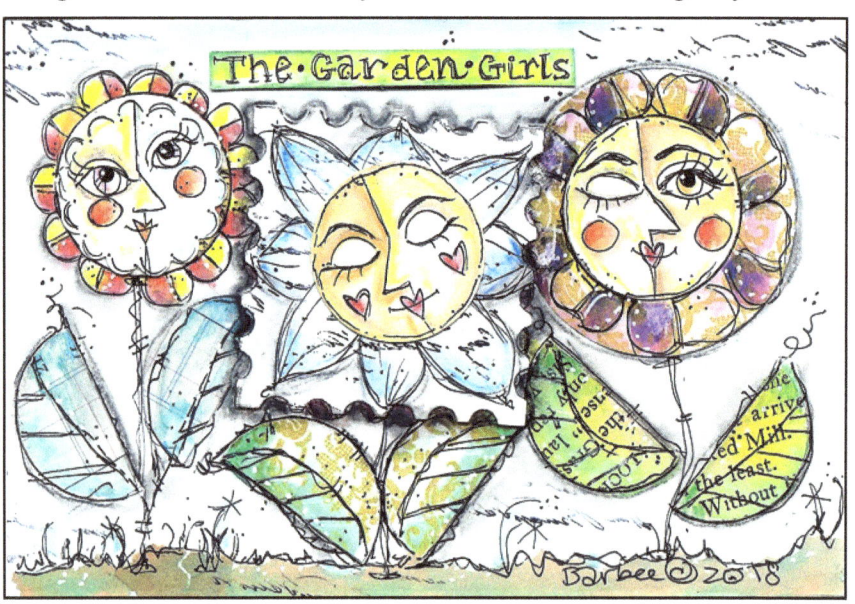

29 for 29 June: PATISSERIE

Jumping around a bit since I'm behind but will try to do more than 1 per day! This prompt was patisserie, typically a French bakery / pastry shop. Here are some characters I cooked up for this card. These cakes and cupcakes love their little cake stands which tend to add to their personality. It's my shop of course, so I added my name and title. Lots of flowers out front plus some random stamping finish things off. I used watercolor, watercolor pencils, black permanent fine point pen, white paint pen. I also used a blue stamp pad so that the background stamp blended in with the background paint.

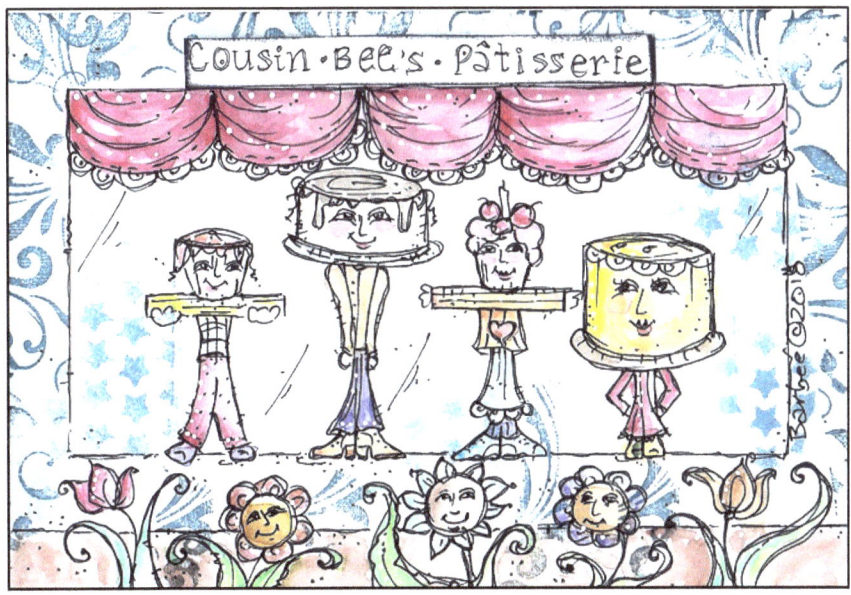

30 for 30 June: TARO OR PLAYING CARD

I used to watch a classmate in high school draw in an illustrative style and one day saw her draw an old man in a robe and hood holding a long walking stick in one hand and a lantern in the other. After talking with her I found out she was copying a card from a deck of tarot cards. When I looked at the tarot cards, I fell in love with the dark fine point pen that outlined, shaded and added texture and depth to each card. I also loved the way that drawing with a pen offered an opportunity to color (I love to color), so I began refining my drawing to resemble that style. That was more than 40 years ago! I also always loved drawing suns, so selected the sun tarot card to draw for this prompt. I simplified it for time's sake but had fun with it. It signifies material happiness, fortunate marriage, and contentment, so felt right to me. I used watercolor pencils and black permanent fine point pen.

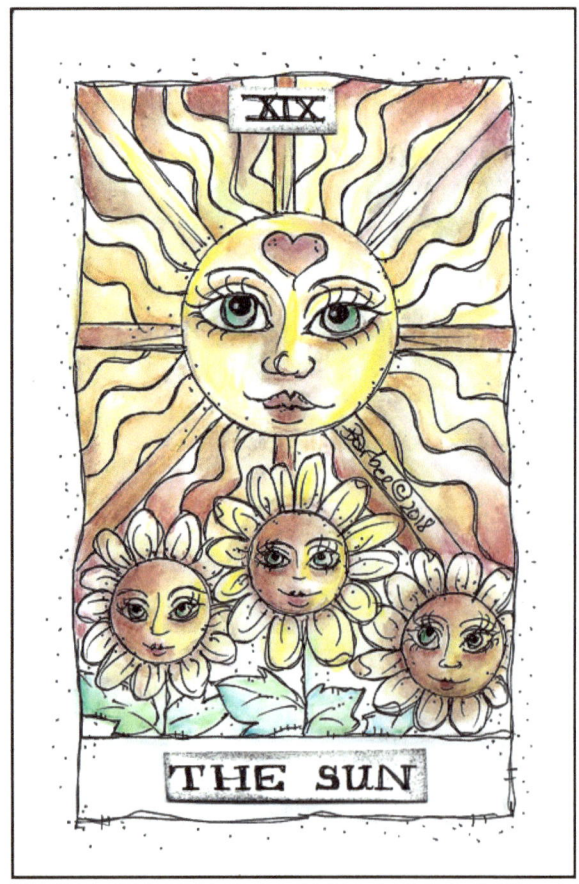

31 for 1 July: CURTAIN

I was trying out shading with watercolor but fear I shaded too much and incorporated my thoughts of dieting in this poor princess! She looks a bit thin, emancipated even, and obviously doesn't sleep well! I decided to post her anyway as I needed to move on to another day and another card. I used watercolors, a fine-line black permanent marker with a bit of white paint pen to accentuate things with dots.

Tip 37: Strive to be perfectly imperfect. Don't fret over small imperfections, but rather enjoy the uniqueness of your art.

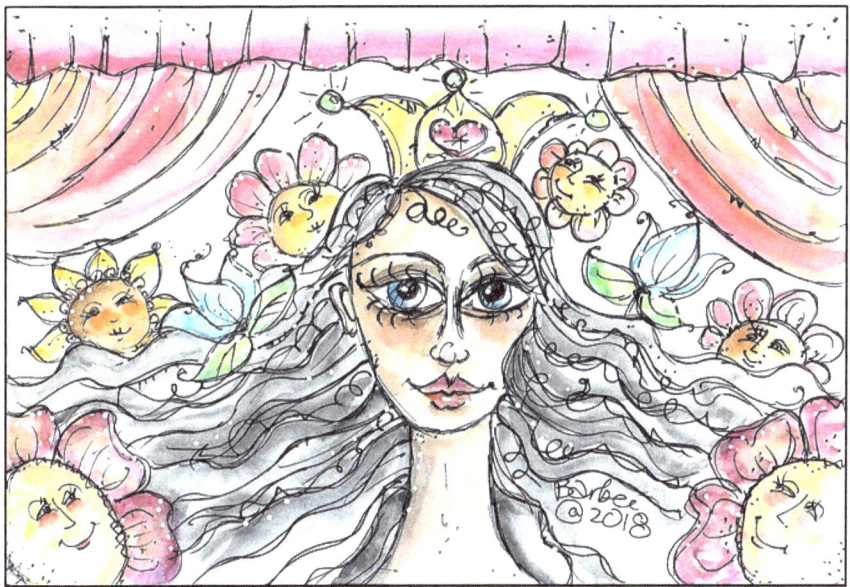

32 for 2 July: COMPASS

This is a compass "mandala." I added a sea scene to honor the millions of people who've used compasses to explore the world and seek better lives. Mandalas don't have to be perfect, and I learned this technique from one of Tammy's daughters a couple years ago. Although I admit I used a circle template, you can sketch a circle and place lines around it then add any "charms" (doodles) you like. I used watercolors, watercolor pencils, black permanent fine point pen, and white paint pen.

Tip 38: Use plastic templates to draw circles or other shapes, if you'd like to.

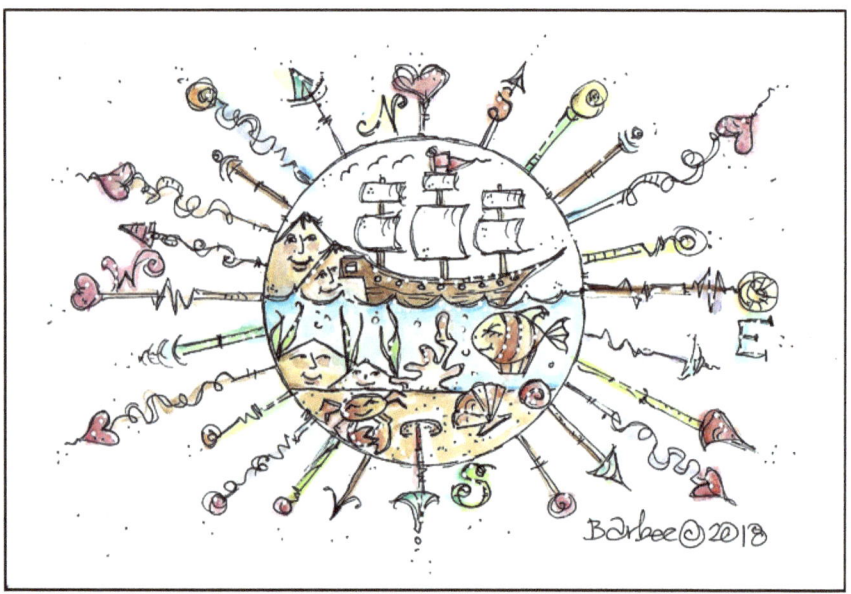

33 for 3 July: DENIM OR BLUE

I call this one: Pig+Cats-Oh!"

Pig and Cat are in the blue-rose period so enjoyed posing for this "blue" prompted card. I considered having them "sew" (as in PigCatSew) but knew it would take longer than I had to make the card. I used watercolor pencils, black permanent fine point pen, and white paint pen. I also lightly stamped a damask stamp with my blue stamp pad.

Tip 39: Use this creative challenge to research some of the great artists of today and the past. Allow their styles to influence your art occasionally, as you may pick up a trait you like.

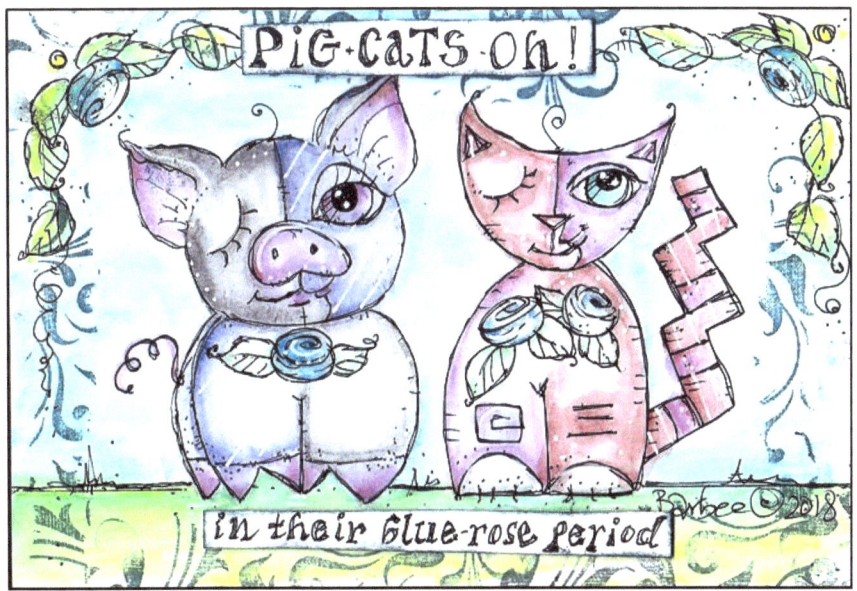

34 for 4 July: PICNIC

Happy Independence Day! It's a wonderful day for a picnic, so these friendly wonkish fairies are carrying along the decorated word "picnic" to celebrate! I used watercolor pencils, black permanent fine point pen, and white paint pen.

Tip 39 from the previous prompt applies here as well.

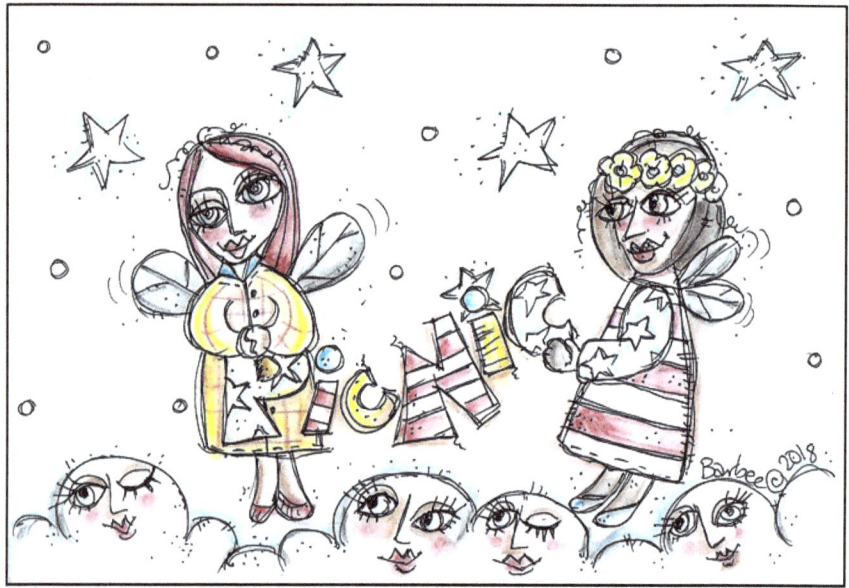

35 for 5 July: MOSAIC

I perused the other "Mosaic" posts in the FaceBook Group and saw several pieces that resembled my ideas so decided to practice wonky, Picasso style faces, instead. I had fun blocking or sectioning off areas, starting with sectioning the card into squares. I then drew a face in each square. I separated the faces with a line where the nose is. I then added dots or lines to different sections. I used a fine point pen, and watercolor pencils to color each area.

Tip 40: Separate a card into equal sections and draw a small design in each section. Drawings may be completely unrelated or related to each other, as in the below drawings of faces.

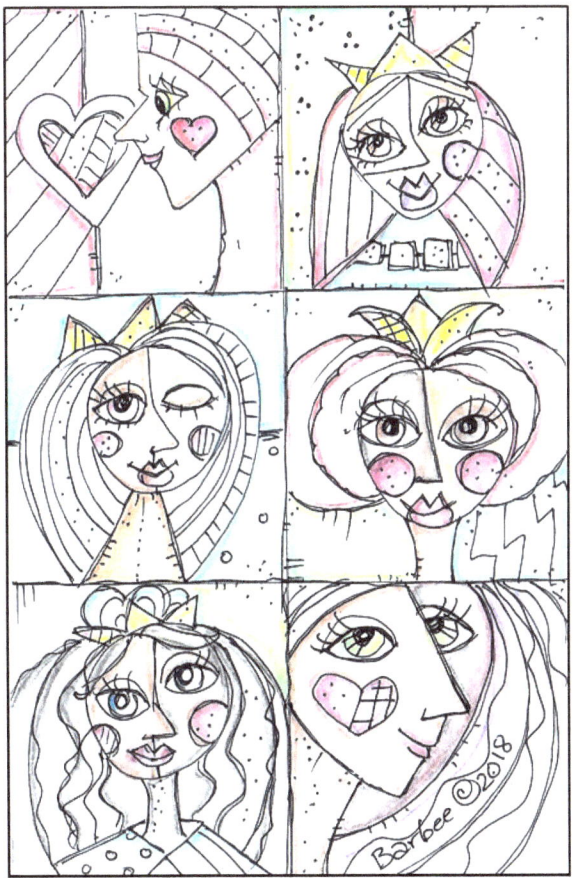

36 for 6 July: PRETZEL

I resisted the urge to look back at a past piece I'd created using the prompt "pretzel," because I wanted to make sure this one was different. I created letters there too, but the letters weren't people! I used watercolor pencils, and black permanent fine point pen.

Tip 41: Draw small random shapes around a card.

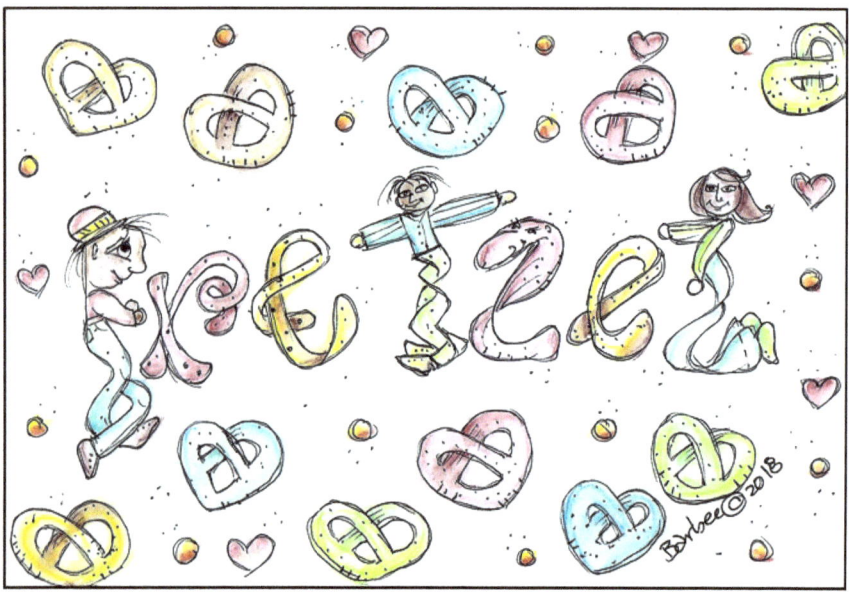

37 for 7 July: POETRY

I wrote a little poem for this prompt:

> Poetry is best read
> On an
> Evening
> That
> Resembles
> Yesterday's best memory.

Notice that each line starts with a letter from the prompt! It's really fun to rack your brain to find a little poem that does that. I wanted to do some loosely painted flowers, so drew, then painted, these forget-me-nots. I liked seeing pencil lines under the painted flowers. I used a fine black permanent pen, and watercolors.

Tip 42: Original pencil lines don't always have to be erased before painting a design. They add texture and interest to a painting.

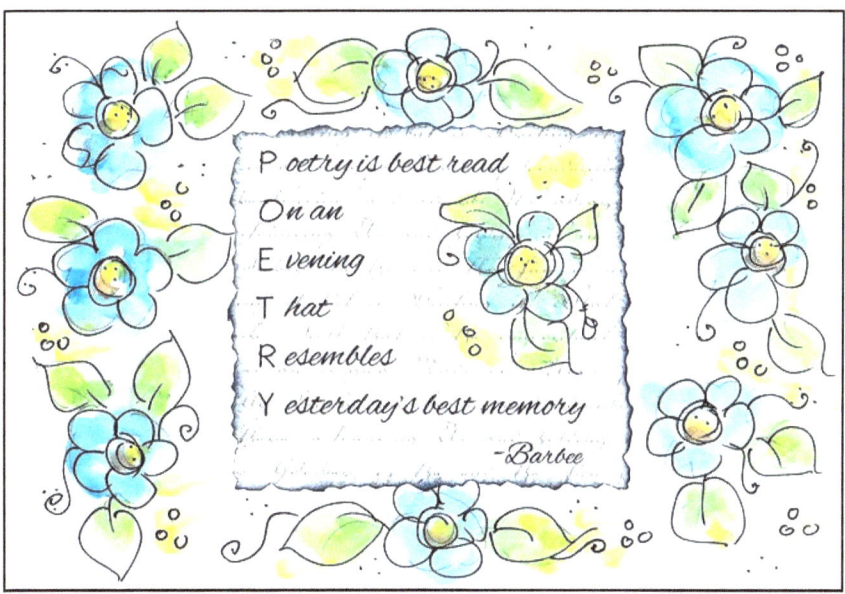

38 for 8 July: PALETTE

Palette girl loves creating art! She's even wearing her Picasso striped shirt, although I used brown rather than black for the stripes. I enjoyed giving her a wonkish, blocky feel. I used watercolor pencils, black permanent fine point pen, and white paint pen.

Tip 43: Vary the colors in your card, even with the same space. The variation adds interest.

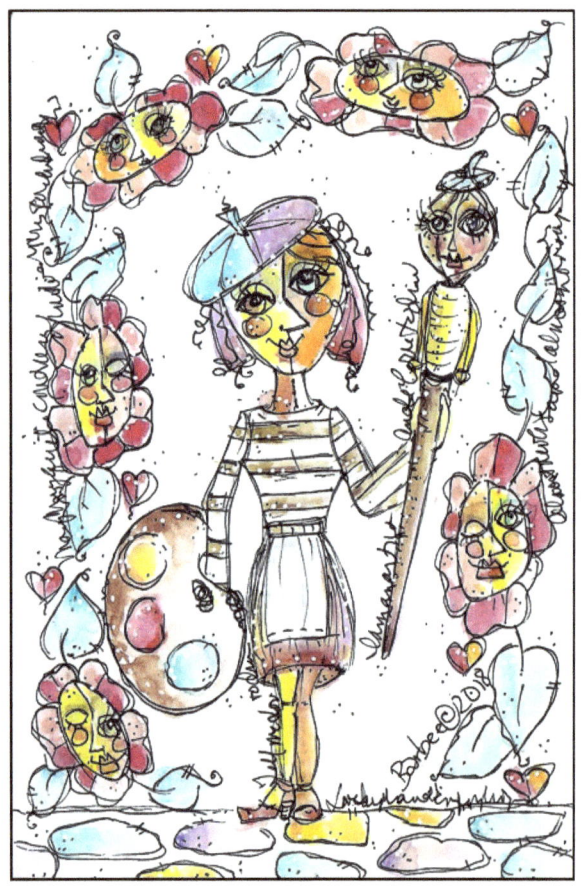

39 for 9 July: PIXELATED

I call this one "Pixelated Faces." I wasn't sure exactly what to do with this prompt but had visions of squares with tiny features in them so just added the word "Pixelated" in the middle and decided on yellow and black for a basic color scheme. It was actually quite fun to add the faces in various colors - flesh, light brown, yellow, gold, and charcoal. I used watercolor pencils, black permanent fine point pen, and white paint pen.

Tip 44: Once you've developed a design, select a few colors to be the palette for your card. By picking the colors before you start, you'll be able to quickly complete the card.

Tip 45: Create a border on your card by adding lines and drawing within the lined sections.

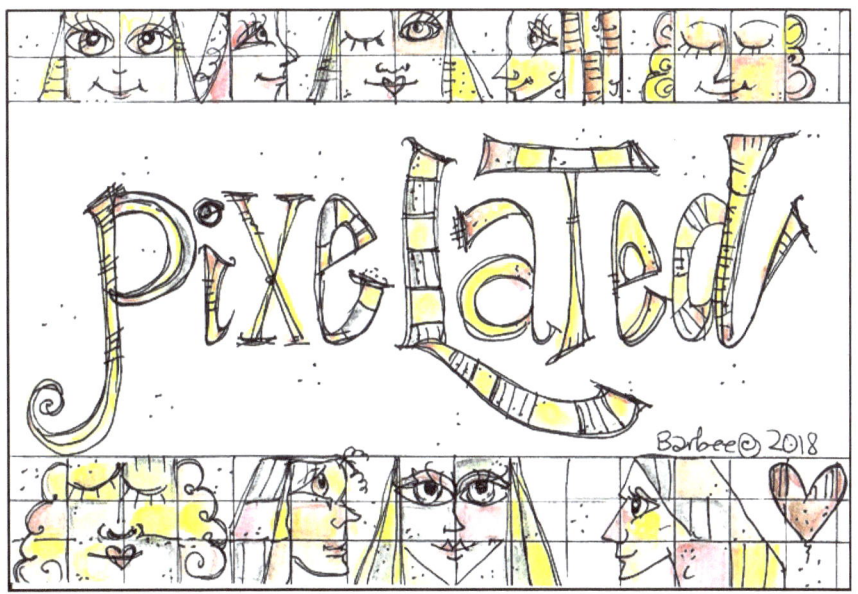

40 for 10 July: PINBALL

I love playing pinball but drawing a pinball game would take way too long, so I drew these pinball "friends" instead. I added a numbers stamp in the background, because what would pinball be without numbers? An interesting factoid I read in popular mechanics was that pinball machines were illegal from the 1940s to the mid-1970s in most of America's big cities because it was perceived to be illegal gambling, robbing children of their lunch money. The article said that just weeks after the attack on Pearl Harbor, the New York mayor issued an ultimatum to the city's police to round up pinball machines and arrest their owners. They rounded up thousands and dumped them in the city's rivers! This card portrays a kinder, gentler pinball atmosphere. I used watercolor pencils, black permanent fine point pen, and white paint pen.

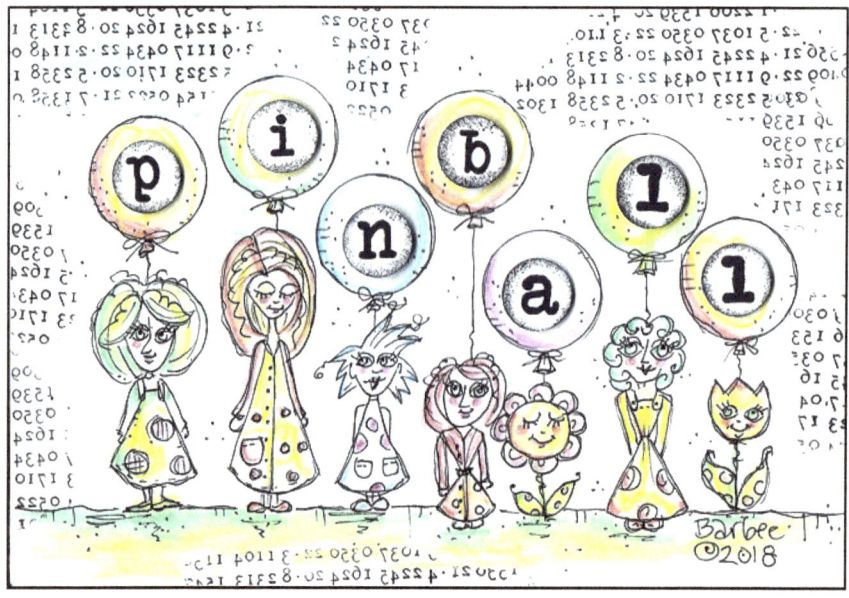

41 for 11 July: PORTRAIT

Creating pretty faces is always fun, but I decided to kick it up a notch by adding sections and coloring lightly on this face loosely inspired by the great artist, Pablo Picasso. I appreciate most of his art but gravitate to those that match my idea of beauty. I've watched a few good videos about him, and he led an amazing life. He also inspired many things in our current lives in the fields of art, architecture, fashion, home decor, etc. I used watercolor pencils and black permanent fine point pen to create this "portrait."

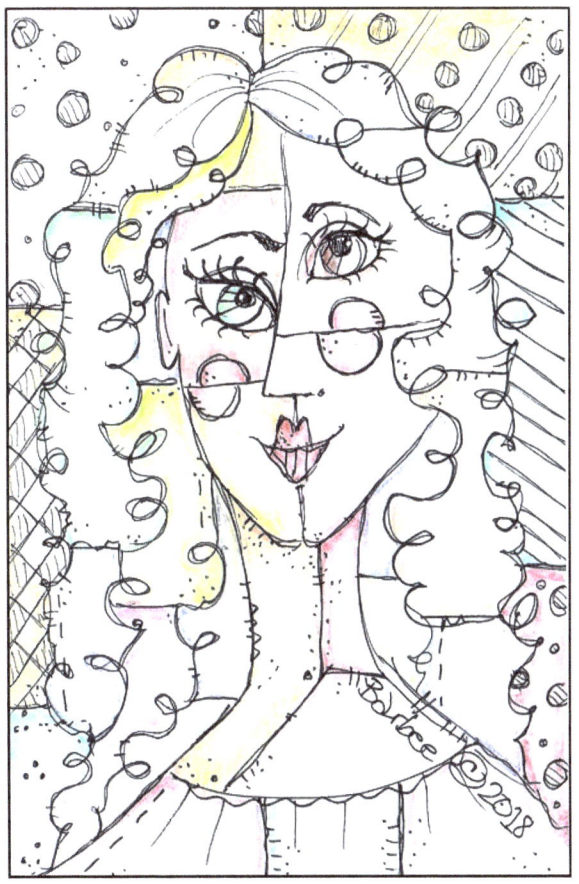

42 for 12 July: PLATE

An appropriate prompt, since we just bought a motorhome and needed to outfit our new motorhome with, among many other things, plates! I know that Corel holds up good on the road but don't like boring, white plates (which figures, since I don't leave much white space in my art! I found a great new Corel line that incorporate 1950s colors and flowers, so am giving them a try. They're called "Happy Days." Of course, Ms. Plate would be lonely in this world all alone, so I gave her a handsome Mr. Musketeer Saucer, and he's the perfect partner! I've been taken by Picasso's Musketeer art during this challenge, so think we'll probably be seeing more of Mr. Musketeer in the future in my art. I used watercolor pencils and black permanent fine point pen.

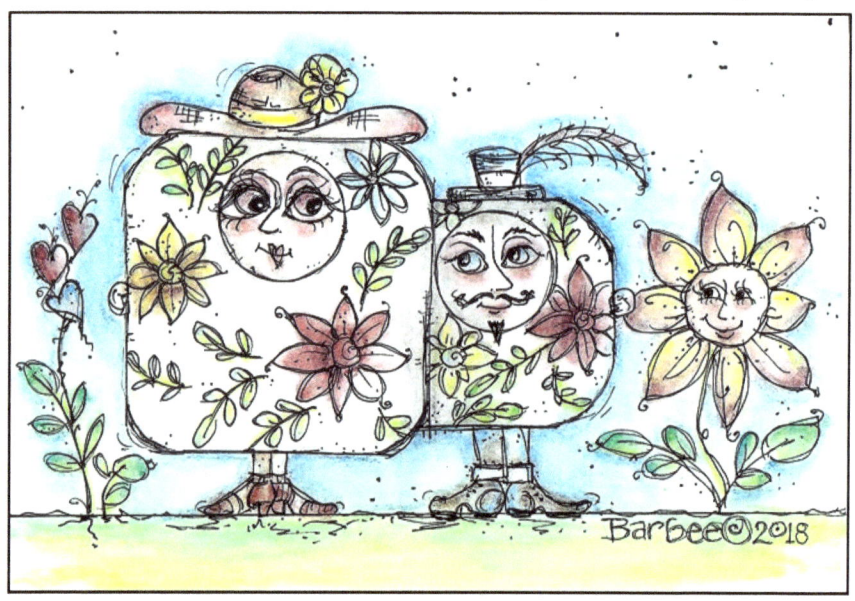

43 for 13 July: WINDOW

These were inspired by old printer trays that held letters for printing presses. I enjoyed drawing lots of windows from which to see all the happy houses, trees and plants. I used watercolor pencils and black permanent fine point pen.

Tip 46: Create uneven spaces on your card as a foundation, then draw objects within each section.

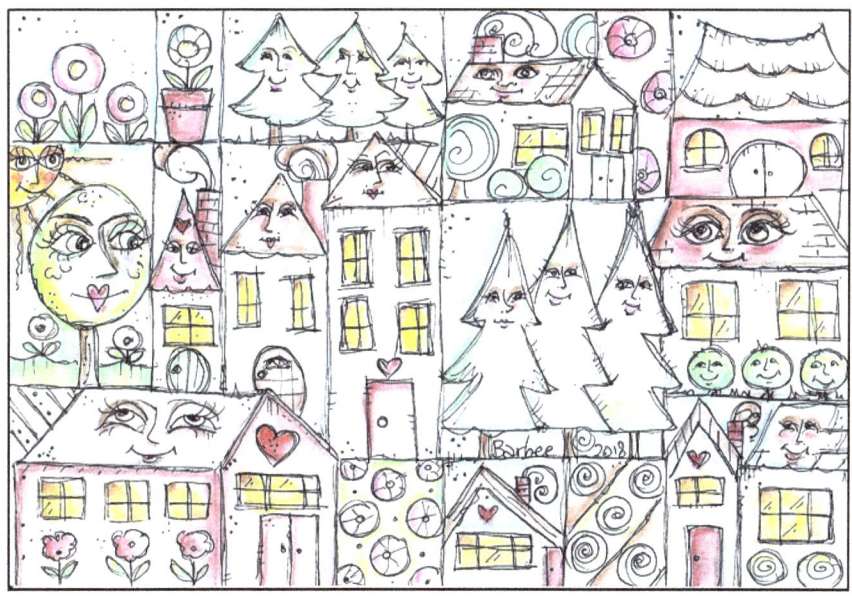

44 for 14 July: FRINGE

When not sure what to do for a prompt, I rely on faces / people to get me through, though even that was a challenge with this prompt! I gave this "Girl with a Quilt" a fringed haircut and a pink and green quilt. It's always fun trying to improve coloring and blending techniques with pencils, although this one took a long time because I was attempting to go against my impatient nature and color very lightly. I began thinking that regular watercolors (not watercolor pencils) might've been a better option, since they can color more quickly. I used watercolor pencils, black permanent fine point pen, and white paint pen.

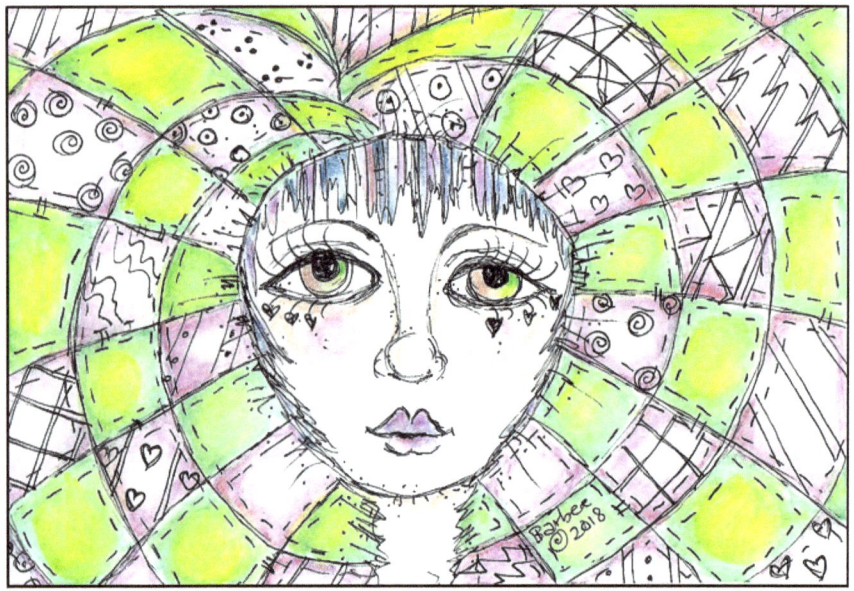

45 for 15 July: CANDYLAND

In thinking about the prompt, my favorite candy, 3 Musketeers Candy Bars, came to mind, so I did a quick sketch of my version of these three guys. I located an early 1960s video advertising this candy and, coincidentally, its byline was: wrapped in stars in CANDYLAND by Mars (Mars is the company that makes the candy). I know that there were 4 Musketeers in the story, but I'm just portraying 3, since only 3 are on the candy wrapper. I sketched this drawing with the finest black permanent micron pigment pen I've ever used, called a 003 (.15mm), because the faces had to be very small to fit on my index card. My process typically is to start a sketch with pencil, then add a first layer of linework with pen. Next, I erase pencil marks, and lightly color with watercolor pencils, using a water pen to blend the colors with water. Lastly, I add another layer of more detailed linework. Sometimes, I add a few brighter watercolor pencil marks and use water to blend.

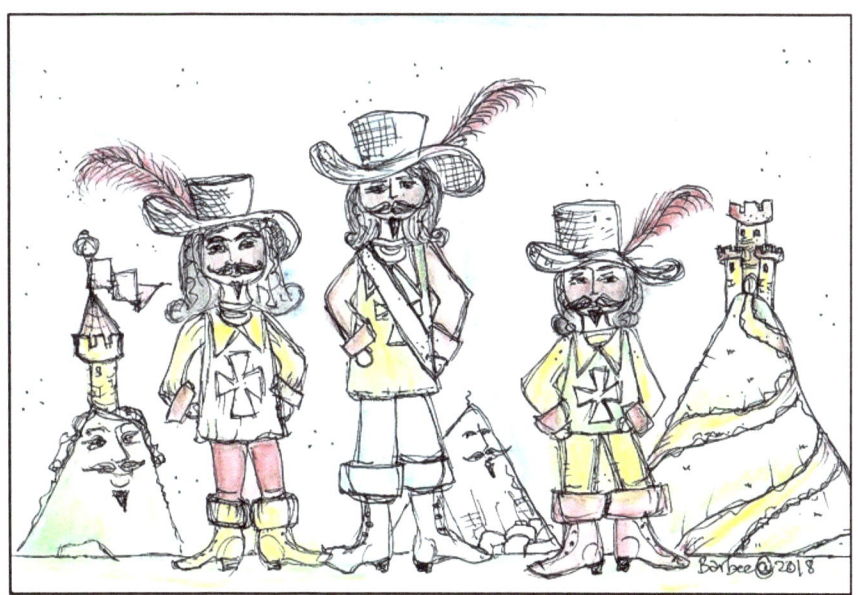

46 for 16 July: TIE DYE

Here are my "Tie Dye Butterflies!" I love adding faces to unsuspecting shapes so enjoyed adding faces and other human traits to these colorful butterflies in an attempt to make them symbolize this prompt. My kids grew up with scary movies where dolls, like Chucky Doll, had awful faces and chased (and worse yet, killed) human beings. These movies made faces and dolls seem scary! I used watercolor pencils, black permanent fine point pen, and white paint pen.

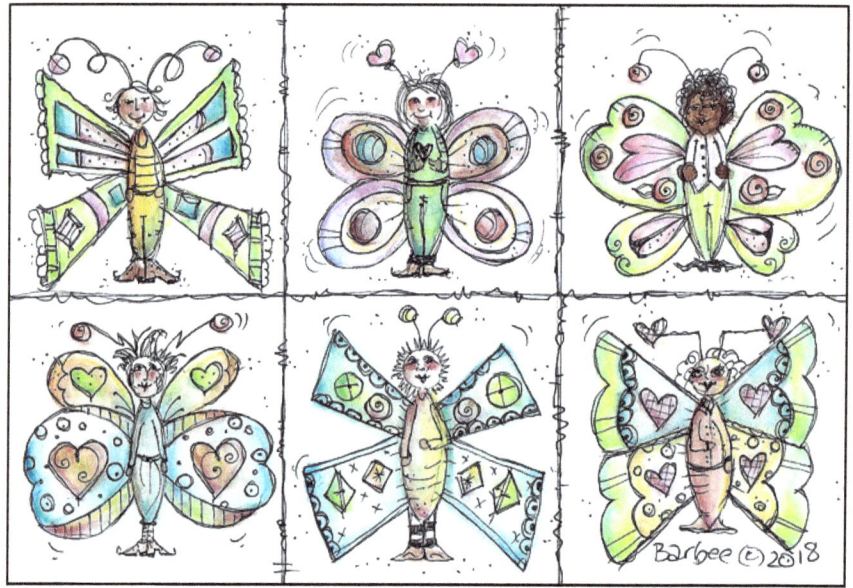

47 for 17 July: LOVE

I call this "Love Doodle Jam" because it is a grouping of things I love to doodle. I used a fine line black permanent pen then lightly colored each item with watercolor pencils, going over some items a second time with the pen to add details.

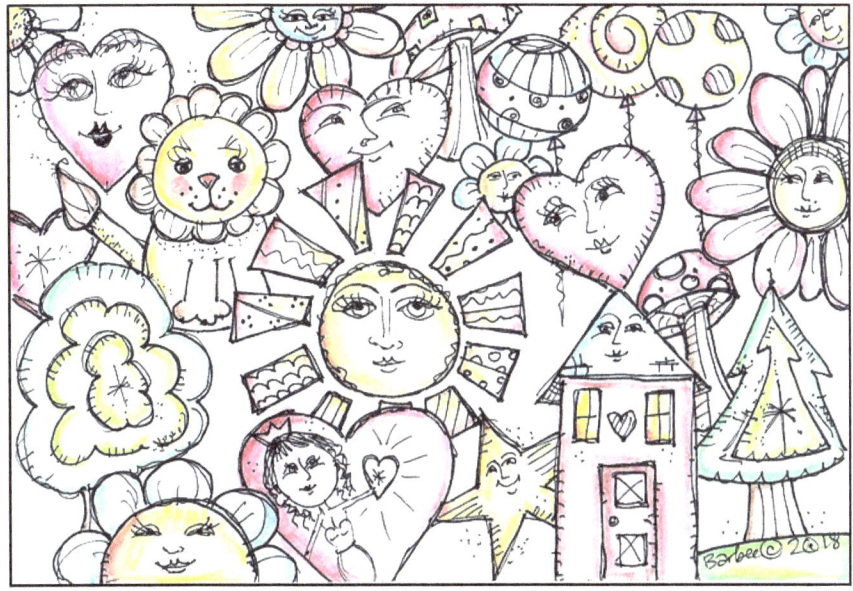

48 for 18 July: CAMERA

My mother used to drive us crazy by taking lots and lots of pictures! Now I'm happy to have so many of my childhood and, for better or for worse, I have become that mom who takes photos ad nauseam. I hope one day my family appreciates them all, haha! Somewhere around the time our youngest son was in college and preparing for a trip overseas, I reminded him to take lots of photos. He told me he'd heard someone say you should take pictures with your eyes and more fully enjoy the moment you'd normally try to capture with a camera. So, I decided to start with HUGE eyes and build a smaller face, along with some little camera drawings scattered around. I sketched these with two different thicknesses of black permanent fine point pen, the larger first, the thinner after. I then lightly colored them with watercolor pencils.

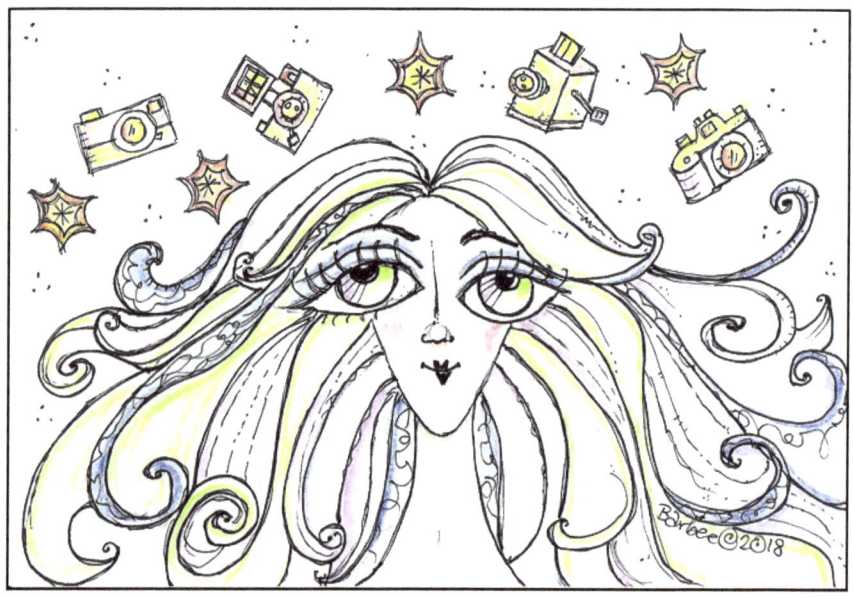

49 for 19 July: LANDSCAPE

Lots of faces adorn this happy little landscape. Every tree, mountain, animal, and of course the sun, appear to be getting along and enjoying a beautiful day, realizing that this is how life should be. I used watercolor pencils and black permanent fine point pen.

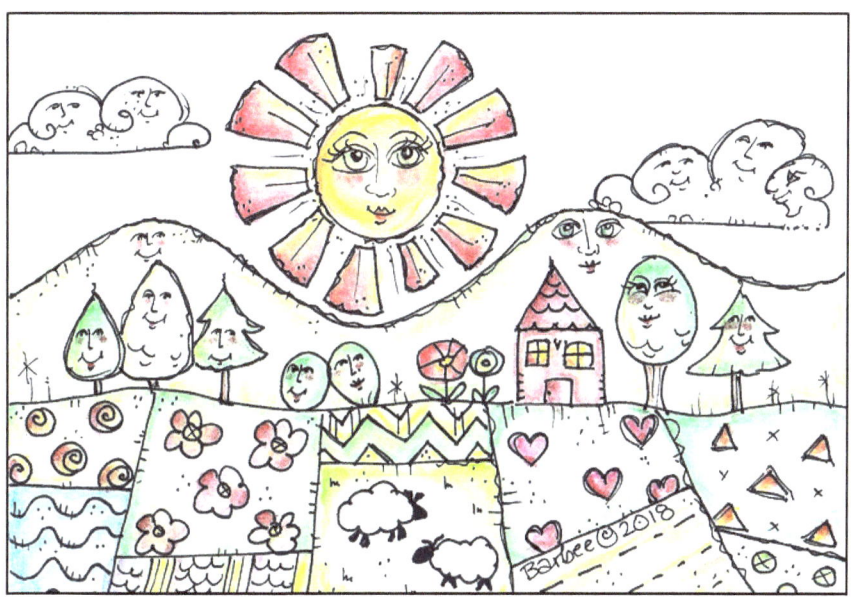

50 for 20 July: RADIO

I call this one "radio waves!" I wanted to stick with the prompt "radio" but didn't feel like drawing a radio so drew a tree where the bottom line of the leaves resembles radio waves. This allowed me to draw lots of little houses on the tree as well as faces all around! I used watercolor pencils and black permanent fine point pen.

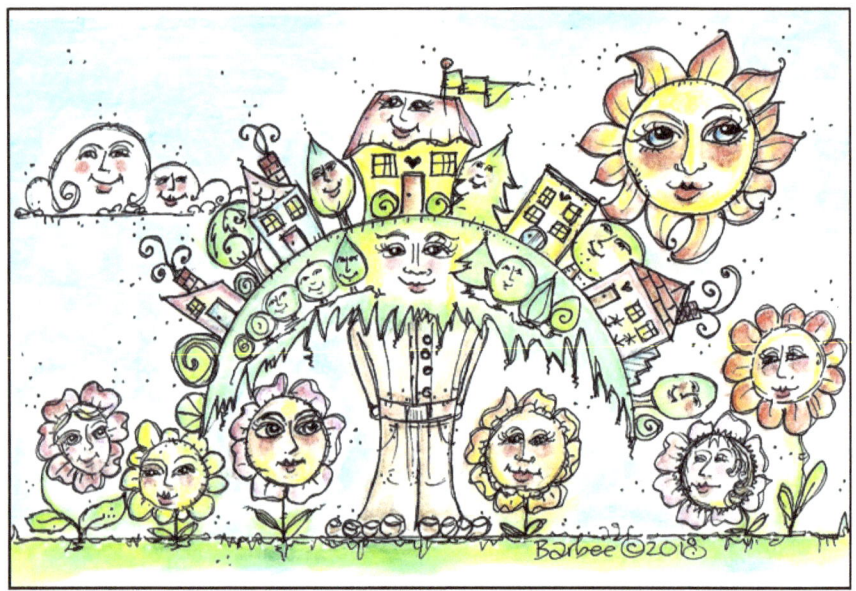

51 for 21 July: MINT

I call this card "Mint and Julep Birds!" We used to live in Northern San Diego County and had mint growing like a weed on one side of the house in the back yard. It used to annoy me because we couldn't get rid of it! Year after year we were invited to our friendly neighbor's house to celebrate the Kentucky Derby. As we walked in, we were greeted with several rows of beautifully decorated Mint Julep drinks - it was a southern tradition. Mint was welcomed in this house! I drew a non-traditional Mint Julep glass on this card, so that I could exaggerate the stem with my little characters! I also added a couple of summer-y birds, Mint and Julep. I used watercolor pencils and a black permanent fine point pen.

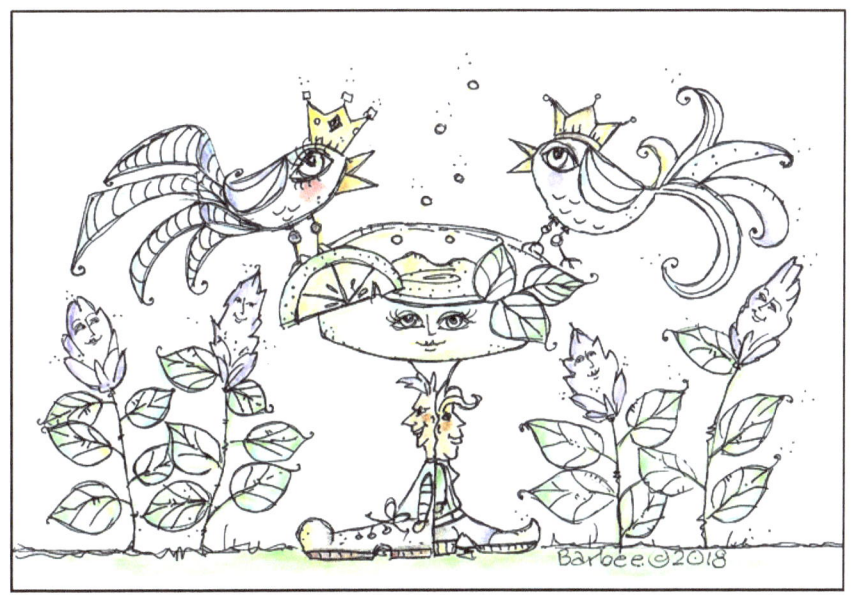

52 for 22 July: POSTAGE

I die cut one of my 4x6 index cards with a die that resembles a postage stamp for the top layer of this two-layered card and drew this postage-related scene of a bird flying a happy envelope to a lucky person on the other end. I used a fine line black permanent pen to draw the first layer, and a finer pen to add some details, then colored it with watercolor pencils which I went over with a water brush to blend. For the bottom card, I used a swirly stamp with a blue stamp pad. I affixed the top piece onto the bottom with double sided tape. I added some light script stamps and a bubble stamp here and there.

Tip 47: Use die-cuts or cutout pieces of paper as a top layer adhered onto a bottom index card for a two-layered card. I already had this postage stamp die and a die cutting machine, so it was the perfect match with the prompt!

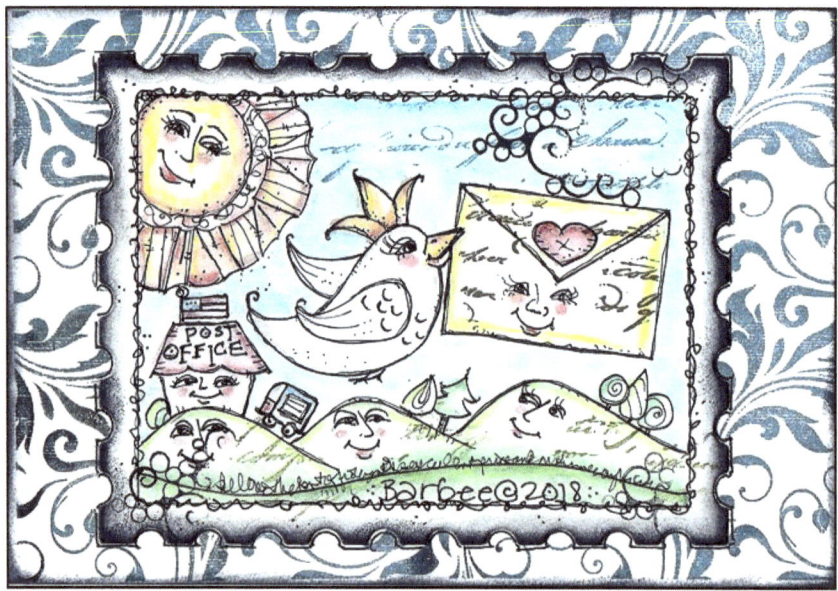

53 for 23 July: CASSETTE TAPE

I had a hard time coming up with something for this prompt but then thought how cassette tapes and cassette players (boom boxes) went "hand in hand" so decided to draw them that way. Of course, I made the player a dashing musketeer while I was at it! I figured that someone on the sidelines watching them dancing and having fun was bound to be saying "Oh no, they're at it again!" So, I stamped that out and glued it to a piece of old book page, then to the bottom of the card. I used a permanent fine point black permanent pen to draw the first layer, colored it with watercolor pencils (which I went over with a water brush to blend), then added more details with a finer black pen.

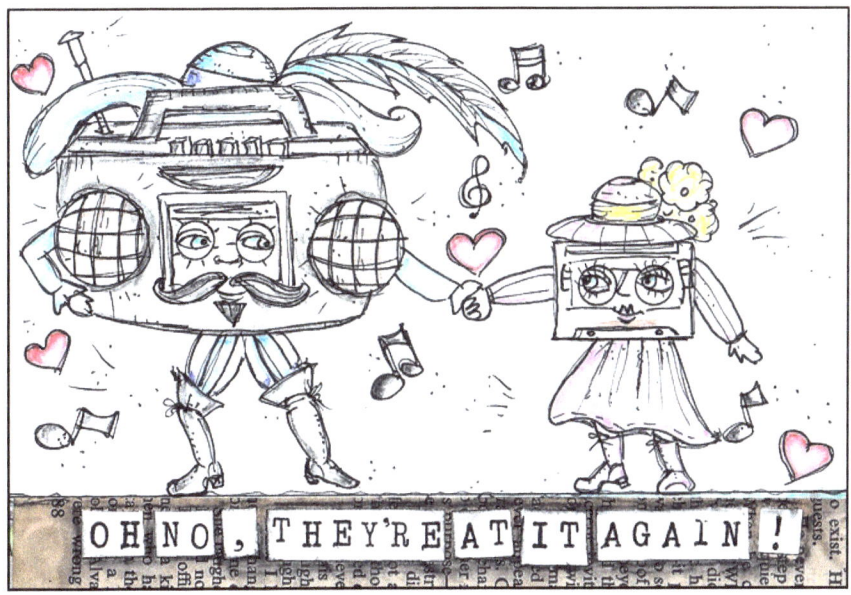

54 for 24 July: TIDE POOL

I call this one (Tide) Pool Party because of the explosion of fun among the little sea creatures in this mandala-like creation! Yes, some who are non-tidal have snuck in too, and together they're having a great time. Well, as long as everyone's still full from their previous meal, I'm sure they'll all be friends! I used watercolor pencils and black permanent fine point pen.

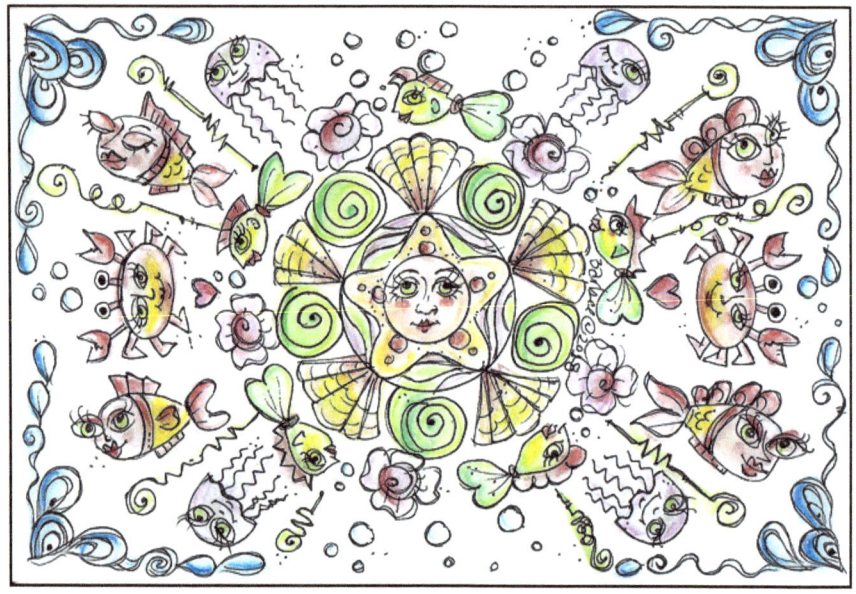

55 for 25 July: CIRCUIT OR NETWORK

I found some vintage circuit diagrams (schematics) and diecut a butterfly and a dragonfly from them. I thought what a great couple they would make, and soon the theme, along with a little story, formed:

> "Forbidden Love" ... He loved every inch of her delicate but strong circuitry and she loved his starry face, muscular wings and fancy musketeer-look. They cared not about the ignorance of others but loved each other equally, never looking past their similarities to their differences and the problems that might arise as they began their life of love - together!

Everything except the faces were lightly painted with acrylic paint. I stamped the background with a couple of random stamps and a blue stamp pad. I adhered the butterfly and dragonfly, faces and mountains to the base card. I used watercolor pencils, black permanent fine point pen and a white paint pen on this card. Lastly, I adhered the words and heart onto the card.

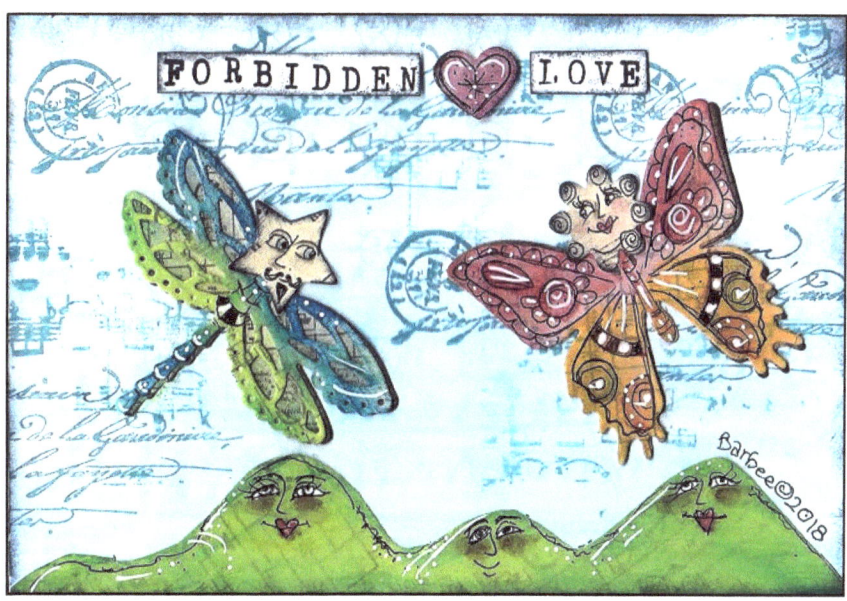

56 for 26 July: TYPEWRITER

In order to write the prompt on this card so it resembled keys on a vintage typewriter, I stamped the letters with a letter stamp then used a half inch punch to punch each letter. I wanted to draw at least one more pretty face before this challenge ended, and then thought I'd save time by drawing flowers. That took longer than I expected because of the layers of detail. I used very soft, light watercolor pencils which required several layers to show up.

Tip 48: For the letters, if you grasp the paper with the punch and center the letter within the circle of the punch, you can draw a circle with a fine point pen before punching to mimic vintage typewriter keys.

Tip 49: Draw and color to please the camera or scanner if you're going to capture and post your creation digitally, as there may be differences from what you see and what the camera or scanner sees!

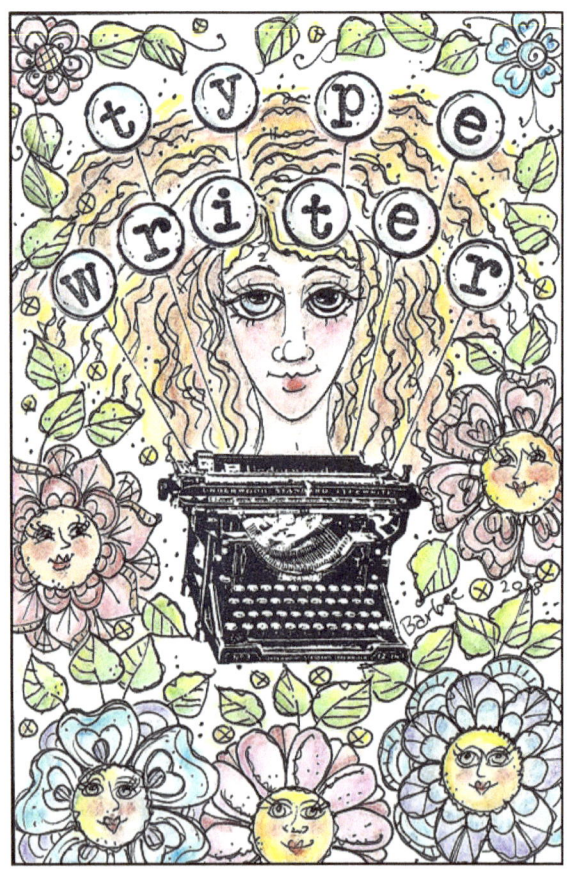

57 for 27 July: TWISTER

I wanted to keep to the prompts but allow myself the freedom to use variations, synonyms and even antonyms of the prompts in creating my daily index card art. In this case, I decided to make twisted lace on a fairy's pretty dress (I call her Fairy Rose) as the main theme. I also wanted her to hold a tasty cupcake. And what better theme could there be for that cupcake than Fairy Rose's dearest love, Musketeer-man! Hopefully it's not too morbid, haha, as it's merely a representation of the mortal musketeer-man she loves.

I sketched this in pencil then erased the pencil lines and used a permanent fine point black pen to ink it. I colored it with watercolor pencils and used water brush to give it that soft watercolor look.

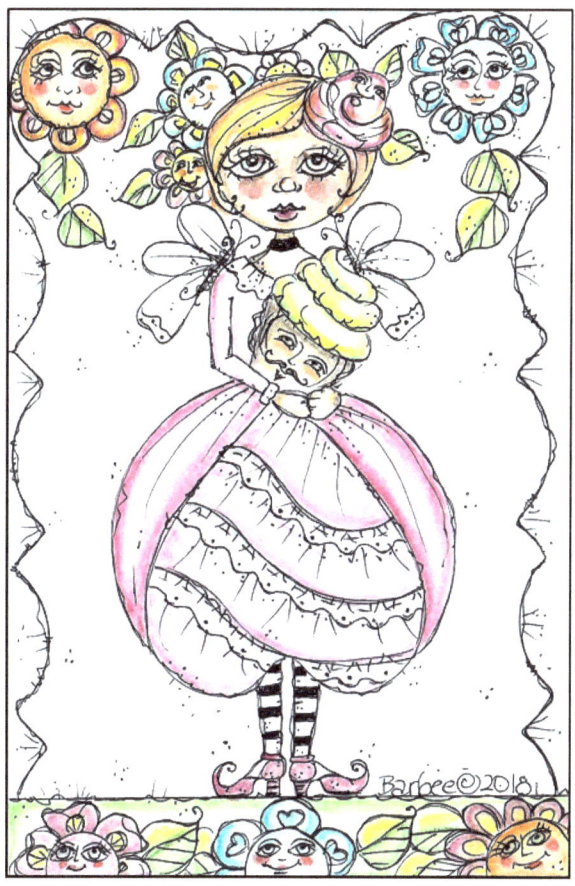

58 for 28 July: FAVORITE COLOR

Think Pink!! Pink and red are favorites of mine, but I love all colors, so I hope I never have to really choose.

I sketched this in pencil then erased the pencil lines and used a permanent fine point black pen to ink it. I colored it with watercolor pencils.

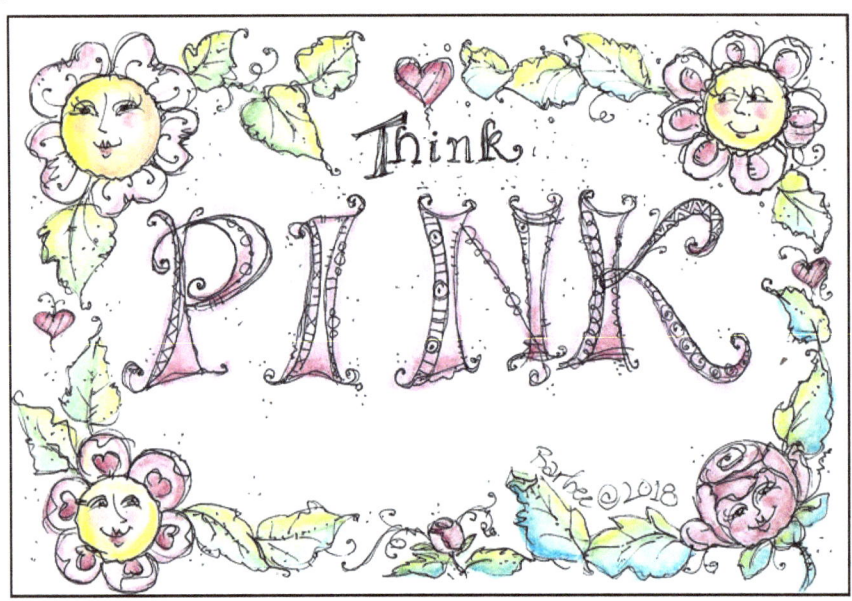

59 for 29 July: STAPLE

I was going to draw a stapler for this prompt, but since I wanted to add one more Musketeer-Man to my 2018 index card collection, decided to draw a man because men are a staple for us humans. Here's a quick definition of "staple" as used in this context: a main or important element of something. Well, that works for me!

I sketched this lightly in pencil then erased the pencil lines and used a permanent black fine point pen to ink it. I colored it with watercolor pencils.

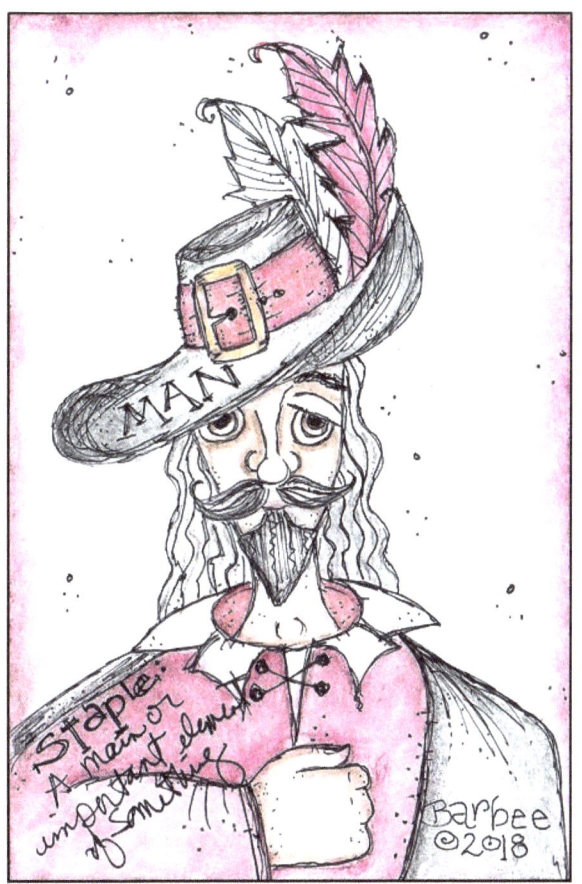

60 for 30 July: WISH

It occurred to me that not only are wishes free, but you can wish for crazy big things and it's just as free as if you wished for tiny things! So, I wrote this on her crown, just in case she forgets: "Extra-large wishes cost the same as small wishes!"

My wish for everyone reading this is that all your big and small wishes come true exactly when you want them to!

I sketched this lightly in pencil then used watercolors to basecoat it. When dry, I added some watercolor pencil. I used a black permanent fine line pen to finish it off.

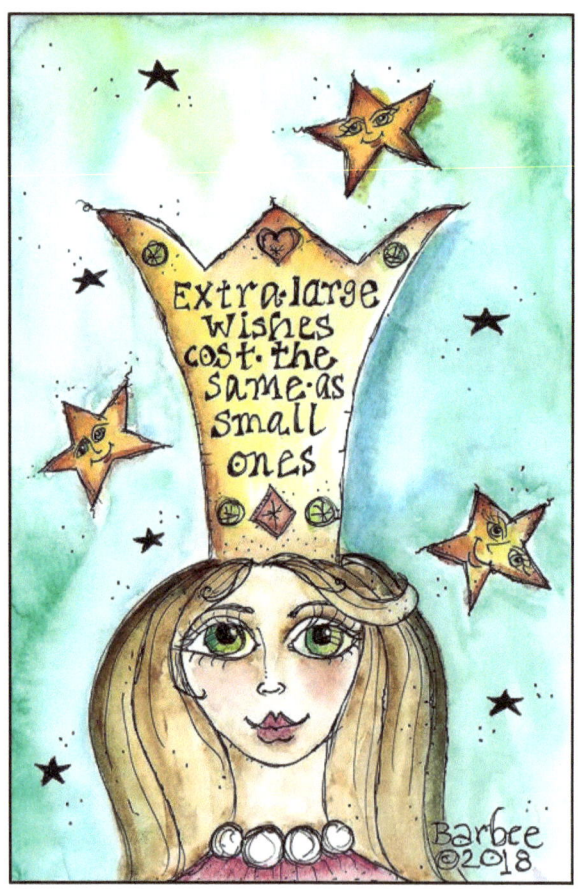

61 for 31 July: TELESCOPE

Here's the last index card for 2018! Drumroll, please ... I did a blue fairy who's thanking our ICAD Guru, Tammy Garcia, for hosting this wonderful creative challenge once again! Tammy's invested a piece of her life organizing, arting, filming, and administrating this event, and I thank her from the bottom of my heart and hope she'll do it again next year. My blue fairy is also thanking the fine admin ladies who helped things to run smoothly in the Facebook Group!

Lastly, my blue fairy is helping me thank every artist, friend/relative and all the Facebook Group members who've supported and inspired me to finish all 61 cards (plus a cover card) this summer! The marvelous likes and comments in the Facebook Group helped me in many ways! I hope to see everyone next year and, in the meantime, hope all my friends make lots of EXTRA-LARGE wishes and lay down plans to have them come true!

I sketched this lightly in pencil, then added details with a permanent fine point pen. Next, I used watercolor pencils to color it, then, added a few more details with my black pen where the pencils muted lines.

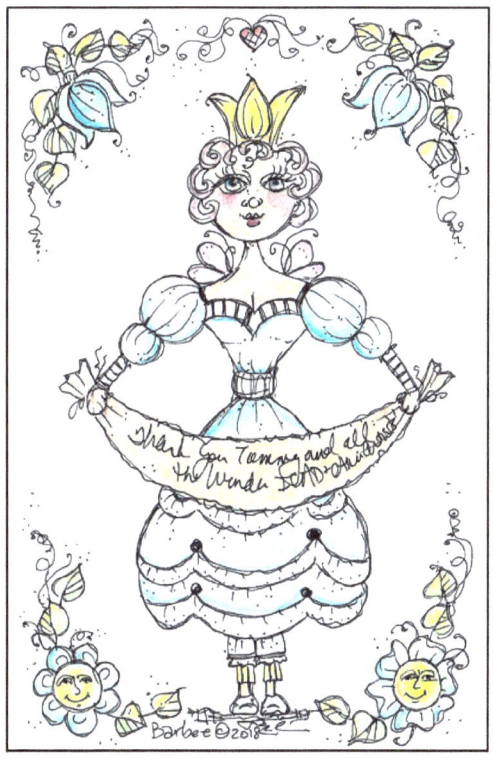

PREVIEW OF BOOK 3: COMPANION SKETCHBOOK

The sketchy image in black and white below was derived from my Roller Coaster index card shown earlier in this book. Although slightly smaller, its appearance is similar to sketched pages contained in my companion sketchbook (Book 3: Companion Sketchbook for Book 2). You can do more than just color it with colored pencils! You are encouraged to sketch additional lines and add your own doodles and other art using a black fine liner pen plus truly alter it by adding some rubber stamps. Along with colored pencils, colored gel pens and markers, a simple fine point black gel pen works great or you can invest a little more money and buy a disposable technical/art pen, such as a Micron Size 01. The sketchy images were derived from my final drawings, so they are not clean black and white lines, but rather sketchy art, sometimes with occasional light gray shading, making them have a sketchier appearance than art in mere coloring books. This will take your arting to another level and enable you to practice not only coloring but sketching too. I hope you enjoy altering this unique sketchbook and utilize the wonderful opportunity it gives you to practice. Everyone's result will be different.

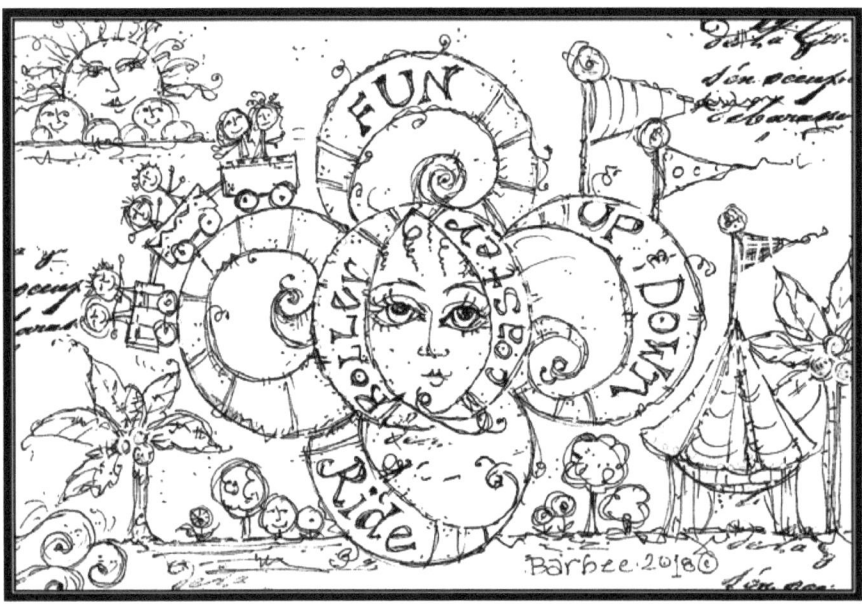

THANKYOU for Picking Up My Second Book!

I hope you enjoyed this book! I also hope you've added some fun doodles in the blank areas of it and that you'll try out my next book, the companion sketchbook to this one, titled: Book 3: Companion Sketchbook for Book 2, 2018 Index Card Art. Remember: the more you practice art, the more you will learn to be happy with it.

If you enjoyed this book, please also try my first book as well, "Book 1: 61 Days of Barbee's Index Card Art," available online as a paperback or inexpensive Kindle book for download to your smart phone, Tablet or other device. It has the same fun style of "happy art" with a positive vibe.

Arting is a verb – an action word and a wonderful way to escape from life's worries, while still enjoying so many wonderful challenges! Be sure to check out and subscribe to my blog at: BuzzyBarbee.blogspot.com and my "Barbara Hauenstein" YouTube Channel as well as those of the wonderful artists I mentioned in the Dedication, Tammy Garcia (DaisyYellowArt.com) and Carolyn Dube (AColorfulJourney.com).

www.ingramcontent.com/pod-product-compliance
Lightning Source LLC
Chambersburg PA
CBHW040229220526
45473CB00001B/168